The *Good* HUSBAND

Glenn & Mary thanks for initial read & comment,

The *Good* HUSBAND

50 Practices
That Will Make You Nearly Perfect

Danny

Danny Langdon
Inspired by Kathleen Langdon

Printed in the United States of America

ISBN Paperback: 978-0-9913975-5-6
ISBN eBook: 978-0-9913975-0-1

Cover and Interior Design: Ghislain Viau

This book was written for husbands.
It is also a love story that this husband, Danny,
has for his wife, Kathleen.

Contents

List of Practices

Preface

I've written a number of books (most, technical and one memoir), but this was the most fun and meaningful book I've penned. As a husband, when you really respect and love your spouse as much as I do, I can think of no other task more enjoyable and rewarding than writing about the wonderful relationship we have. It was her idea and encouragement that both initiated and motivated me to write this book. She apparently thinks I am a great husband and thought other husbands could benefit from my apparent wisdom.

I've stayed away from the topic of husbands as fathers. Fathering is so complex that it deserves a book itself, and I leave that to another to write. This book concentrates on your role as a husband and, of course, I usually mean a male partner. Having said this, the practices are equally applied, if perhaps in need of some adjustment here or there, for partners in the gay world (which I profoundly support).

I asked my partner, Kathleen, to read the draft manuscript several times, and to add content where the practices needed a woman's perspective (e.g., menopause). While the content of this book represents my perspective on being a good husband, I wanted to make sure it was in alignment with how women think about men, as well as what practices they appreciate their husband demonstrating in partnership. She helped clarify the usefulness of the content of this book and also honed some of the practices. She is the good wife who is loved and so appreciated by what I hope is her good husband.

Finally, much appreciation to my good editor, Roby James. She has adjusted to me through several books with great patience. Special thanks to Ghislain Viau of Creative Publishing Design for his excellent work in book cover and interior design. He works with both efficiency and attending to the writer's desires. Thanks to my niece, Kristen Puckett McKenna, for her very useful "opinions." Also, thanks to my granddaughter, Brittney Langdon, for help in several dimensions of getting the manuscript in order. I think her words at the very end of the writing and editing express pretty much what this book is intended to achieve:

"I really enjoyed the book. I hope that if someday I am to find someone to share my life with, they will read this book so we can have the best relationship possible."

Men

You are not expected to learn and master all that is suggested in this book. But if you adopt a few new practices, you will be certain to enhance your relationship with your partner. The author wishes you all the best. Live and learn as the wise old sage once said. Or as Maya Angelou said:

"When you know better, you do better."

Women

While this book is intended for men, it seemed every time I mentioned it to a couple, as it was being written, the universal response from the women was, "Boy, could my husband learn a few new things. Let me know when you publish it." Expect your partner to practice only a few new things as it is truly hard for most men to change. If he does, reinforce him for improving, and you'll be surprised if he doesn't continue to change in other ways.

Partners

The practices included in this book were written for partners no matter their orientation. Thus, each person has within their role a multiplicity of practices they do or do not perform. Although written for men, the practices included here are not universally or exclusively limited to male or female. Thus, I trust whatever role you occupy, you'll learn new practices that you and your partner can benefit from.

Introduction

This is a book written for guys, but women are just as likely to benefit from its content.

The content is designed to increase awareness of the ways you and your partner relate and negotiate—called "practices"—to promote a vibrant relationship. These practices may remind you of 1) what you used to do, but stopped; 2) are continuing to do, but should not; and 3) may never have done because you never learned, but really oughta wanna.

These practices promote a form of clarity in your relationship so that you can better communicate, support, and value one another. A word about clarity. You know how difficult it is to navigate in fog and how much better a clear, sunny day is? If your marriage/partnership is fog-like (that is, blurry communication full of eye-rolls and shoulder shrugs, anger flareups of unknown origin, marked by a lack of joy or fun), then getting more "clarity" will bring improvement on many fronts.

The description of each practice will include specific directions or suggestions on "how to"; yet many are pretty self-evident. That is when and where awareness comes in. You need to remind yourself of what needs to be done to continuously enhance and maintain the relationship. (Yes, you will need to remind yourself to get flowers now and then!)

The 50 Practices are not listed in any order of preference or importance. Of the 50, some are obviously more important in your relationship than others; it is for you and your partner to decide. I am of the mind (and personally emphasize in my relationship) that the ability of both partners to process (Practice #14) is key to a successful relationship. I have found from my experience (through two marriages) that partners need to possess, or more likely in most cases develop, a highly functional way of processing needs, situations, arguments, and all the decisions that manifest in your joint effort. I know that it took years of mistakes, learning, practice, and even unnecessary arguments before I got it right (and still sometimes I need reminding).

There are, in addition, to mastering processing, several related practices that you should be especially attuned to and use. Effective processing between the two of you requires attention to practices such as As Aretha Said, R-e-s-p-e-c-t (#5), You Can Ask for Help (#8), Viva La Brain Difference (#9), You Can't Change the Other Person (#11), Avoid Nitpicking (#19), just to mention a few. You will find, as I have, that once you are able to process virtually anything without hurt feelings or unresolved issues, and with some compromise and workable solutions, recognizing both sides' feelings, you can process anything together. Once there, you will like one another so much more and feel life is fulfilling as a couple. Others will recognize that you do and wish they could. Attending to the practices in this book will help, I am sure.

As you read you should identify which practices speak loudest for improving your relationship. I suggest you use Appendix B, which is a listing of all the practices in the book. You can check off which you do well, which you need some work on, and perhaps there is even one or two that don't particularly apply to your partnership. Then review each practice with your partner in meaningful discussion, sharing your points of view. Perhaps together, you can read one practice each week and discuss it. The two of you can commit to working on those that need mutual attention and improvement. For example, when I learned that my partner needed more Listening with Empathy (#13) from me, our discussions went more smoothly, without hurt feelings, and resulted in workable solutions. Try it. Practice can make perfect.

Have Your Song

A song—your "own" song—can convey how you feel emotionally about your partner. Since most of us are not songwriters, we can rely on those who are: composers and lyricists, poets, artists who speak to you both. Your very own song will always remind you of your feelings about each other.

It might be true that wives are genetically more sentimental than husbands. (I happen to be pretty sentimental, so I feel like I am one step ahead on this particular practice.) It's also true that most women express their emotions more easily than men do. So, any way in which you can understand your partner's passions—and show her that you do—can be very important. And I learned that having a song for the two of us is a way to say "I love you," and "I'm thinking of you," and "Aren't we wonderful together?" and maybe even, "I'm the luckiest guy in the world" all at the same time, without having to find the words myself.

You can do this too, by following a few simple guidelines. Before you begin, however, think about the kind of things your partner likes rather than thinking just about the kind of things you like. It's possible that they already talked about what songs really warm their heart—and perhaps you don't remember—but if you do, great. If you don't, you may want to pay more attention, or even ask them directly to see if your tastes agree. If they don't, it's best to lean more to what they want.

Now to the guidelines. First, I suggest you look for a song that really touches your partner's soul—not so much in a spiritual way, but in a sense that the song moves ones soul in powerful ways, whether because of the melody, the lyrics, the voice of the singer(s), or all of those. For example, one of my sisters and her husband chose as their song "Could I Have this Dance for the Rest of My Life?" As you can tell from the title, this song captures how they see their present and future life. Since my sister was a dance teacher for 40 years, one is not surprised that "dance" in the song title is a clue to what she might be drawn to for a favorite.

Next, look for a song that is personal to both of you, preferably one that imparts a message of love. Country and Western songs are very often delightful for their passion and down to earth wisdom about relationships (though I would not recommend such titles as "Your Cheatin' Heart" or "Please Release Me.") Some better songs in the C&W genre are those such as "I Walk the Line," "You Are My Sunshine," or "I Love You Because You Always Understand, Dear." There's a longer list of both types at the end of this practice, but it's by no means exhaustive!

If you both agree on a song (and while I'm not convinced the Ohio State fight song qualifies as a love ditty, if you both love it, go for it!), then adopt it. And if you need to browse some romantic songs together, to see what your choices are, try one of the many websites dedicated to romantic songs, such as *https://bestlifeonline. com/romantic-songs/* or see my list at the end.

 ## Scenes from Our Relationship

❖ My wife and I have our song of life, love, and even death, "Loving Her Was Easier than Anything I'll Ever Do Again," written and performed by Kris Kristofferson. We sense that the lyrics speak to how we feel about one another both emotionally and physically, how we move together in the world, and the impact we have on each other's being. My wife says that, upon hearing "our song," she turns into "a puddle of awe!" And as I sing and play that song on my guitar, it's clear to me that I mean every word of it.

A few love songs worth considering:
- ❤ Ring of Fire by Johnny Cash
- ❤ Make You Feel My Love by Bob Dylan
- ❤ Love Gets Old by Wouter Kellerman

- ❤ In My Life by Judy Collins
- ❤ At Last by Etta James
- ❤ La Vie En Rose by Edith Piaf or Daniela Rose

Songs To Be Avoided:

- ✖ I'm Movin' On
- ✖ It Wasn't God Who Made Honky Tonk Angels
- ✖ Making Believe
- ✖ Please Release Me
- ✖ Singing the Blues
- ✖ Vaya Con Dios

Actualize Your Vows: "My Connubials"

Married or committed couples make formal vows to each other. These are important words, and they deserve to be actualized throughout our lives together. I call the things we do to keep the vows alive and contributing to an ongoing relationship "My Connubials."

W hen people form a serious relationship with one another, they generally make certain commitments which take the form of vows or promises recited in some public forum, whether it's a religious venue, a Justice of the Peace's office, or someplace like a National Park. Some couples use vows from a particular cultural group, and some write their own, so the promises they exchange as they begin life together can vary substantially in wording, meaning, and impact.

One of the Christian varieties goes something like this:

In the name of God, I, [groom's/bride's name], take you, [groom's/ bride's name], to be my [husband/wife], to have and to hold from this day forward, for better, for worse, for richer, for poorer, in sickness and in health, to love and to cherish, until we are parted by death. This is my solemn vow.

Personally, I am far more impressed by the Hindu vows, recited as the bride and groom walk around a flame honoring Agni, the Hindu fire god:

Let us take the first step to provide for our household a nourishing and pure diet, avoiding those foods injurious to healthy living.

Let us take the second step to develop physical, mental, and spiritual powers.

Let us take the third step to increase our wealth by righteous means and proper use.

Let us take the fourth step to acquire knowledge, happiness, and harmony by mutual love and trust.

Let us take the fifth step so that we are blessed with strong, virtuous, and heroic children.

Let us take the sixth step for self-restraint and longevity.

Finally, let us take the seventh step and be true companions and remain lifelong partners by this wedlock.

Other cultures provide different vows, and many couples draw from the ones that speak to them as individuals. For example, the Apache marriage blessing can be inspirational for people with a strong connection to the natural world:

Now you will feel no rain, for each of you will be shelter for the other. Now you will feel no cold, for each of you will be warmth to the other. Now there will be no loneliness, for each of you will be companion to the other. Now you are two persons, but there is only one life before you. May beauty surround you both in the journey ahead and through all the years. May happiness be your companion and your days together be good and long upon the earth.

Treat yourselves and each other with respect and remind yourselves often of what brought you together. Give the highest priority to the tenderness, gentleness, and kindness that your connection deserves. When frustration, difficulties and fear assault your relationship, as they threaten all relationships at one time or another, remember to focus on what is right between you, not only the part which seems wrong. In this way, you can ride out the storms when clouds hide the face of the sun in your lives—remembering that even if you lose sight of it for a moment, the sun is still there. And if each of you takes responsibility for the quality of your life together, it will be marked by abundance and delight.

For certain, there is ancient wisdom in all forms of vows promises. In light of all these, I suggest there should be every day, living "connubials" throughout a relationship which recognize the continuing relevance of the vows from the time when the couple made a commitment to one another. That those vows are remembered and that are an important part of the couple's life together.

In general, husbands may forget the vows more quickly and more thoroughly than wives do, so I am suggesting that husbands look for ways to make the connubials part of the relationship—ways such as noticing when to make a wife's life easier, safer, or happier. Some examples of potential connubials may be:

- She needs something fixed—Be her guy for that.
- She's misplaced something—Try to be Mr. Finder.
- She's fed up with the kids' crying—Be Mr. Kid Magnet and entertain them.
- Her car needs gas—Be Mr. Gas Attendant and get it filled up.
- She needs cash—Be Mr. ATM.
- She wants takeout—Be Mr. Pickup.

You can always find connubials if you stay aware of what your partner needs. They're not difficult, and they bring rewards. Not finding them can have unwanted results. Recently one of our friends needed to take an important business trip that required a 50-mile drive to the airport and then a week's stay in another city. It was only when she was getting gas for her car that she realized her husband had borrowed her ATM card and left her with no way to get money for her trip. I see him as a man who left his connubials at the altar and did not think of ways to help his wife. We were not surprised to learn that they divorced shortly after she got back from that trip. It seems he had failed in many connubials.

 **Scenes from Our Relationship**

❖ My wife is a fair driver—not great, but okay, and we both know it. Therefore, when she sets out to participate in one of her many activities (such as meetings at church, a social event, to serve on a board, or the like), I ask if it would help if I drove her there. She often declines, but, for example, if she wants to have a drink or if the roads are slick from rain or ice, I make sure she knows that I want to be sure she'll be safe.

❖ In like manner, if she is preparing handout materials for a meeting or wall hangings for her artwork, I can help make Xerox copies or attach the hooks and wires accordingly. She is free to say no to any and all these offerings, but also to say yes or ask freely for others that match her needs. Accepted or not, she knows that I am thinking of her well-being. When she says *that would be nice of you to do so*, I often respond, "Yes dear, it's just one my connubials!" And she kind of chuckles knowing that I care to be of service to her.

Humor in Relationship

After physical attributes and general personality traits, most people seek a partner with a sense of humor. Why? Well, humor is much more than "being funny." It is more about seeing life's absurdities. Humor allows you to kid each other, bring levity to unlikely circumstances, and help one another overcome annoyances or fears.

Humor doesn't come naturally to everyone, so it may take a little time, effort and practice to develop. You need a mutual understanding that kidding around is not criticism of your partner, or the circumstance they may be facing. If humor isn't innate to their character, you may have to explain what you're doing a few times along the way. They may have to be patient with you. If at any point you are the only one laughing, better to back off, recognize that a joke or jibe isn't working, and move on. Sometimes saying something silly can create an absurdity all by itself. If you need practice, start with a friend or coworker, keep it light, and bring what you learn into the important relationship with your partner.

Humor doesn't mean just telling jokes, nor sharing silliness on TV. It demonstrates that you can see circumstances that are truly absurd about life in general. It can arise in the very act of living your life, because life is too important to always take seriously. When you enjoy it, you can find parts of life very funny indeed. When you look at something that could be scary and see what's absurd about it, you break its hold over you and your partner. You confirm that much of living is just not to be taken all that seriously, so you find ways to make light of it together.

There are a couple of guidelines that will help make humor a rich experience as part of your relationship. First, the laugh is best when it is not at anyone else's expense – especially not your wife's. Jokes or sarcasm that seem to lessen your partner's worth are hurtful to them and harmful to you. Second, let the humor happen naturally, because being open to events of life that can be funny and recognizing them together will enrich your lives and enhance your relationship.

Laughter is a human process and a human need. Laughing at the same things together makes life easier.

 **Scenes from Our Relationship**

❖ I made a mistake on a recent vacation. We were slated to visit a South Pacific nation consisting of 85 islands, and I booked (unknowingly) a hotel reservation for the first four nights on the wrong island. We arrived shortly after midnight to be told our hotel was nowhere to be found on the island that we had landed on. We were tired, and my wife might have been upset, but I remarked that at least I got the right country, which made us both laugh, and something that could have been really annoying was suddenly just a minor snag. It turned out to be an adventure we will never forget as we end-up staying someplace else that was marvelous. We laugh about it now every time we recall that trip.

❖ Another time, after a long morning of work and errands, we both fell asleep on the couch. I woke up first and watched my wife sleep. I sometimes do this because it makes me smile to see her resting when she is usually so active. She opened her eyes and asked me why I was watching her. I told her I enjoyed seeing her sleep, because she isn't nearly as surly as she is when she is awake. I could do that because we were not in public, and because her surliness—which is rare—is a running joke between us.

❖ I wear glasses. Have since the third grade. As such, I keep a fleece cloth near my computer whenever I need to clean them, which is often. The other day I noted it wasn't there when I needed it and asked my wife if she knew where it was. She said, and I quote, "Yes! It walked over there onto the counter where I needed it" and she said this with a straight face. "How convenient," I replied. No accusatory explanation or response was needed. That was funny.

Start the Day Together: Knock Three Times

Starting your day with a practice you and your partner both like is a great way to ground yourselves in your relationship before the hustle and bustle of life takes you in separate directions. A signal helps you begin the day with each other.

*S*tarting the day off right is important, because it can set the tone for the entire day. Waking up with affection and optimism can help everything in your relationship to fall into a comfortable place because you and your partner are in sync in the morning. After the honeymoon phase of a relationship, it is easy to fall into routine, but find a way to show you love each other every morning, and even the routine can be lovely.

Now I can hear you saying, "But I haven't got that much time in the morning," or "There are the kids!" or "I have to shower before I leave for work," or "We're on different schedules," and so on. I am suggesting you find five little minutes to use just for each other. For instance, you could set the alarm a little earlier, or shower more quickly or teach the kids what "our time" means. My wife's parents called it "the arsenic hour"—theirs came at the end of the day, but they made sure they had a chance to be a couple every single day, no matter how many children there were. As they found out, and as my wife and I learned, the rewards can be tremendous when the ordinary has a chance to be extraordinary. Here is how we begin the day:

Scenes from Our Relationship

❖ My wife initiated a ritual many years ago that I am just crazy about. Before we begin the day, we lie in bed and talk about things (plus anything else that we might want to do, if you know what I mean). She is a lark—meaning she wakes early and with energy. Other wives might be harder to get moving in the morning, but mine wakes nearly an hour before I (say around 6:00 am), goes to the kitchen, fixes a cup of tea, does some of her journaling, and starts preparing her own breakfast. (We have found that we each like different things for breakfast and lunch, so we tend to make our own, although on occasion I am known to make breakfast for her). I wake up an hour or so later (we are now both retired), but before I get out of bed, I let her know I am awake—by knocking three times (a reference to Tony Orlando and Dawn 70s song, "Knock Three Times) on our wooden headboard (or wall), so she can hear me. Sometimes I have to do this a few times before she hears me (i.e. the microwave blocks me out), but I don't get up until she hears the knock. If that doesn't work, I stick my head out the bedroom door and let her know I am awake. She then comes into the bedroom, climbs into bed, and says, "Good Morning, dear, how did you sleep?" For variety, she might say, "How is the Angel of my Morning?" or other cute thoughts that come to her. And we snuggle up together, hold hands, and spend the next 10 to 20 minutes just talking about things. "What do you have planned for your day? What do you have planned for me?" "Do you need my help with anything?" No politics, no leftover arguments, or even issues we have to decide for the day--and certainly nothing that would lead to some kind of misunderstanding. It's a great moment in time to remind each other how much we enjoy our life together, how we love the environment and home we share, and any other thoughts that make begin the day together.

❖ I've heard of other successful signals. We have a friend who makes a latte for his wife every morning. Another friend told us that every morning her husband rubs her back as they greet good morning and talk for a while about the day in front of them. It always makes her feel treasured.

As Aretha Said, R-E-S-P-E-C-T

Having mutual respect in partnership (married or not) is a must. What does it look like? How do you foster it between the two of you? If it is missing, what can you do?

love this song, especially when sung by Aretha Franklin. In the movie *The Blues Brothers* it is done with such style that it makes me want to get up and dance. More important, its message for life and relationships is sublime.

We explore a lot of practices in this book that make for a good husband/partner, but perhaps none is more important to a loving, healthy, and ever-deepening relationship than mutual respect. If one member of a partnership does not offer respect to the other, it can create a tension that may be instantly apparent to friends or family.

A lack of respect can be one-sided or mutual (and it might start as the former and grow into the latter). If it exists, it can surface in openly negative ways, damaging the partnership. Its sources can be buried deep in the past. It can stem from one's own upbringing, seeing the lack of respect between one's parents, or it may be the result of parents who told their child that he or she was worthless, creating a lack of self-respect in the present adult/partner. Remember Groucho Marx's famous line, "I refuse to join any club that would have me for a member."

Wherever that lack of respect comes from, it can destroy a relationship and, as a good husband, you must recognize whether you are suffering from it – and fix it. A promising way is to find a group or a therapist to help identify its source and root it out. If it is part of your partner's repertoire of characteristics (picking on you in public; calling you stupid; laughing at your choices, yelling at the kids, etc.), be aware that *you* cannot fix *them*. However, you can be honest with them, telling them that you will always love them, but that some of their behavior is hurtful to you, and that you want them to be aware of it. If they are sorry and want therapy, support them; if the lack of respect is mutual, marriage counseling might be helpful in keeping the relationship together.

I do not suggest it is easy to build respect where it has not existed. But it may be easy to start the process. Begin noticing and reinforcing qualities in your partner which you admire. Are they a good conversationalist? A loving parent? Do they say interesting things? Do they share their talents? Identify what you love about them – or what you loved about them when you first met. Thank them for the times the two of you enjoy.

Respecting one another does not mean you have to be *like* one another. It can actually be helpful if you are different, because you can use those differences to complement each other.

 **Scenes from Our Relationship**

❖ My wife and I are in the same profession, but there are major differences in our talents. We were able to be in business together for nearly 25 years and made it a success. She is a holistic person, outgoing, able to see the big picture. She is creative and a master facilitator. She is also a strategic thinker and a consummate communicator.

I, on the other hand, am a systems person whose main skills are logic, planning, and execution. I get the bills paid on time.

For years, we have appreciated each other's strengths, and we have made certain each of us knew how valuable the other was – and is – to us. I have made it my business to make it obvious to one and all that I admire and respect her. Recently, at a social event in the neighborhood, I was intently watching her interaction with the other people, and my admiration for her must have shown clearly, because I heard one of the other women say to her companion, "Look at him. That's his lady talking, and he's very proud of her."

25

I turned to her and said, "She's got my respect!" I really feel like I have her respect as well.

It took us time and attention to reach this point with one another, but there is no magic about it. Any husband can do it with attentiveness and love.

For Heavens' Sake, Hold Your Partner's Hand

This is an easy daily practice that can bring a couple together. Out for a stroll, in a market, at the movies, you can see happy couples holding hands. Handholding does so much to connect us that it can serve as a barometer of our feelings toward one another.

When I was a teenager, I was so shy that just the thought of holding a girl's hand was downright scary. For the longest time I did not have the nerve to try it, and now I know I missed many great opportunities. On reflection it seems odd that that level of fear could be aroused by something I now think of as so natural and wonderful. The first time I finally dared to reach for a hand (her name was Mary), it was wonderful. We were, finally, in direct contact—one person to another! This touching was so special to me that I thought it was almost as good as a kiss! It took me another few months to dare to get to that wonderful other form of touch, but that too I mastered (also with Mary). Now, I have no problems touching and kissing and holding hands with my wife (only). Indeed, these are some of my most favorite moments in life. I can tell that it makes her feel good, and it really makes me feel great.

Touching, while obviously a physical thing, is really more about the feelings it creates. A huddle in football or a scrum in rugby has a feel to it—it's about comradeship as much as it is about calling plays. An arm around another's shoulder, maybe during a time of sadness, can bring a feeling of closeness and convey support. Words may not be needed at all. Holding a child's hand can make the child feel safe and understand that a parent is wordlessly saying, "I'm here for you." Touch is a human sensation about so much more than the physical that it has been adopted in cultures all over the world as a greeting, a way of making a vow, even a spiritual expression. It pays huge dividends in your relationship with your partner.

Handholding accomplishes a number of things at the same time. First, I hold my wife's hand because I want the world to know that I love her very much. And when a couple is in their 80s (as I am today), it must look kind of cute, because I see people smiling at us all the time. I've found that the more we hold hands, especially in public, the better we feel about one another.

Second, having a very tactile relationship is a barometer of honesty in our relationship. If my wife seems hesitant or uncomfortable when I reach for her hand, I know something is amiss, and it allows me to ask what's wrong. Our relationship is healthier when any negative feelings are brought out into the open, and holding hands is a way of ensuring that we are in sync with one another. This is testable in any partnership; if you stop holding hands after you've established it as a habit, you can readily see that something is "off" in the relationship, investigate it, and resolve any issues you might not have been aware of. And, by the way, hugging at the end of a disagreement helps to let each person know that the relationship itself is still strong.

Third, in addition to telling the world that I love my wife, holding her hand tells her in a clear way that I love her and that I enjoy being with her. We are stronger when we are together.

Scenes from Our Relationship

❖ One of the times my wife and I always hold hands is when we go down the aisle to take communion at our local church. To us—and perhaps to those in the congregation who see us—it is a sign of our life and commitment to each other in the present and perhaps into eternity as well. When she gives me the cup, it is a weekly blessing on our union with one another. An additional church-based instance of touch is when we wash each other's feet before Easter. That action is intimate, emotional, and very highly charged.

❖ Touch has also been clearly healing for the two of us. In 2007 I had an operation, during which I had a strong negative reaction to the anesthesia. As I lay in recovery, my blood pressure spiked dangerously. I told the nurse I needed my wife. The nurse brought her in, and when she took my hand, my BP dropped 40 points almost at once. Touch sustains and heals—and handholding is a way of bringing its power into your life. If you haven't been doing it, I recommend you start.

Pitch In

Is your partner your servant? Take some personal initiative; don't wait to be asked. Offer and do specific tasks that make your shared space special. When you see your partner doing something, find out how you can help.

31

No one person is complete in themselves. No one is perfect, nor able to do everything perfectly well. One reason marriage or partnership exists is to create something greater than the sum of its parts–that is, to meet the majority of life's demands with skill and lots of personal and collective meaning. This means working together to make the best life possible for you both, as well as for children and others you value in your domain.

A major hindrance to this ideal is the division of work of running along traditional gender lines.

In this regard I admit I am very influenced by the image of my mother as I was growing up. And it's not so much because she told me (and she did) to treat women equally, but rather because of what she exemplified. To explain that, I need to tell you about my father. My father died of old age (65 in those days) when I was seven, and I am the last of nine children. At the time of his passing, he was in the scrap metal business and older than my mom by 27 years. His line of work meant that he was in the business of buying used metals (e.g., old farm machinery, motors, junk cars that had seen their day, water tanks that no longer worked, and assorted nuts and bolts). My father had to cut the larger pieces of metal into smaller pieces that could then be loaded onto a railway car and sent to a steel mill for reprocessing. He also bought hides and pelts of animals of various sorts and sent these to other markets like a tannery—remember, we didn't have plastics in those days. He was, by all accounts, what we refer to today in environmental terms, a "recycler." When he died, my mother, having six children still in the house, went to work in the business the next day, because that was her only livelihood for her family. She, too, like her husband, cut metal with a torch, loaded railway cars with iron, processed hides, managed people (always men), and so on for nearly 40 years on her own thereafter. You get the picture. I eventually wrote a book about her titled, appropriately, "My Mother Can Beat Up Your Father."

As the last and youngest child, I used to routinely see my mother go to work around 6:30 a.m., six days a week, wearing Levi's, a plaid shirt, cowboy boots, a bandanna around her hair, and a friction-striker attached to her hip pocket for lighting an acetylene torch. She would come home around 6:00 p.m., face all dirty, with blue eyes emerging from the clean area where goggles protected her eyes from flying sparks. She would take a bath (no shower in our small house), put on a flowery dress, and appear before us children as our beautiful mother.

I used to go to where she worked, about a block away and watch her at times as she did what was for all intent and purposes thought (in those days) of as "man's work." In addition to that work, she volunteered in numerous capacities and was a respected member of her community. She was later honored as Mother of the Year in Idaho and a runner-up in the nation. Thus, as a child I learned that there really isn't a difference between the roles of men and women. And that made me aware that, really, anybody can do any task, which can have powerful effects on a marriage.

A partnership is an opportunity to make every single day a little better than if it were a "go-it-alone" proposition. Housing, food, shopping, administrative tasks, banking, cleaning and communication with family and community are all part of leading adult lives in a developed country. When each person in a relationship (married or not) pitches in, using their abilities, interests, talents, and a shared interest in fairness, the relationship is enhanced. It is better because it offers an opportunity to share in the work of life that is not based on traditional thoughts on gender, family history, or income level.

In deciding who does what, it helps to make sure the work is divided fairly. Washing the clothes, for example, has no gendered characteristics. Anyone can do it. It's a task that essentially involves putting clothes (either white or dark, not both) in a washing machine, adding a certain amount of soap (there are directions) and turning it on (other directions). What could be difficult about that? Oh yeah, you do have to put them in the dryer (more directions) and take them out and then fold them. The same can be said of changing a car tire. Granted, that job may be a little more complex, is usually done on a busy street, and demands some strength and facility with a lug wrench, but it is more than possible for either sex. These examples are indicative of all things anyone can generally be capable of! Why should they be thought of as being relegated to one sex or the other? It makes no sense!

The basics of cooking are really mostly a matter of some practice that your mother (or father) should have taught you. I am not saying here that men should do all the cooking (or any other task usually assigned by societal norms to women). But, at least assume your fair share of it. Surely you can handle a barbecue or turn on a stove, and if you can't, you can learn how (Google and YouTube are your friends). Besides, most of cooking is, at its simplest, following a given recipe that only requires reading directions. Measuring a teaspoon instead of a tablespoon can be learned in seconds. A pinch of something is exactly what is implied. Objects exist into which you can pour a cup of oil or water.

A friend once told me her husband learned how to fix fiberglass on his boat but maintained that replacing a lock on a door was too hard for him! Another friend said he had failed at mastering cooking after two or three decades of trying, but he did master making reservations at local restaurants! So, for you males I am going to make it easy so that you can gain some confidence and immediately impress your partner. I include a simple recipe—see Appendix A—you can prepare. Your wife will delight in what you have done for her—let alone her palate. I've tried, tested, and prepared many recipes (usually found online) that, along with some vegetable or salad, make for a fine, tasty meal. (And don't leave a mess in the kitchen for her to clean up; take care of it yourself.) Once you've tried it, gentlemen, you can expand from there to recipes you find and add to your repertoire— again Google and YouTube are great resources for expanding your culinary skills. You vegetarians can talk to your vegetarian friends and find what works for you.

In conclusion, I am suggesting that the idea that certain things are only woman's work must have been thought up by an early Neanderthal male who wanted to be waited on after a long hard day at the hunt. It has always looked to me like a form of control! Pitching in should really be more an issue of what you will share in your mutual relationship with spouse and with others. And be assured that there will remain some traditional role categories for both sexes—just fewer and more equal in the final analysis.

Scenes from Our Relationship

❖ We are ones to prepare our own meals, so takeout and ready-made meal fanciers may have difficulty relating, but there is an important point to be made about cooking and relationship. On a typical day I am the one to select something from the freezer for us to have for dinner, although I usually confirm my selection with my wife. When it comes time to prepare the dinner, we can usually be found in the kitchen together. I might have put a potato in the microwave for a preliminary four-minute cook and then into the oven, while she is washing the lettuce and making the salad. One of us decides on a vegetable to have with the dinner, while the other sets the table. Someone remembers the water and ice for a drink. In all this, it doesn't always have to be her doing the salad, the water, the table-setting, but rather what presents itself as the meal preparation is underway and climaxes with a fine meal that we sit down (with quiet music in the background) to enjoy together. Rather, it's a pleasurable event wherein each of us pitches in.

❖ Whenever I hear my wife unloading the dishwasher (or some other household task), a signal in my brain (a little Pavlovian, I admit) says, "Why should she have to do that by herself?" So, I get up, walk over, and start helping to put dishes, cups, dinnerware, and so on in their proper places. It's a small thing, but it tells her that I am helping not only with the big things, but with the small things of daily living.

Here's a partial list of tasks that perhaps you are not currently doing but could easily learn to do. Your partner will love you all the more for taking the initiative to help:

Task	Relative Difficulty
◆ Making the bed	Easy
◆ Washing the clothes	Moderate
◆ Buying groceries	Easy
◆ Taking out the Trash	Real Easy

♦ Dropping the Kids off   Moderate (easy to do, until you
add sharing life with them)

♦ Doing a Favor   Easy: Don't say it's hard

♦ Filling the Car with Gas   Easy

♦ Vacuuming   Moderate

♦ Going to a Kid's Games   Easy-Moderate

♦ Making Breakfast   Moderate

♦ Cleaning Leaves from Gutter   Hire Someone

♦ Talking Instead of Texting   Moderate

♦ Etc.   Mostly Easy

You Can Ask for Help

Men generally feel like we must do things entirely on our own. But if we can learn to ask for help, there are positive side effects: Showing a need for them makes our partners feel they are contributing, and things tend to get done better and faster. It can be a win-win!

think men, in general, believe it is a weakness to ask for help – and that's a dumb notion. We will risk going up a 12' ladder without asking someone else to hold the bottom of it steady. We will handle a heavy load and not ask someone else to lift the other end (my current back issues testify to that stupidity on my part). We decide to drive in a certain direction and not stop to find out if it's the right direction (though I'm not guilty of that one!). I could go on.

But asking for help at home is not so much about the act of asking as it is about showing trust and confidence in your partner. My wife has demonstrated on many occasions that when I do ask, she appreciates being needed. Even if she can't fulfill a request, most of the time she can, and she is always glad I asked.

I had to learn that. I used to dislike asking for help at home, even though I was OK asking for directions on the road. I began to realize that my partner really liked to be asked and to help, much as I normally like to pamper her. As I got older (and smarter), I began asking her to help even with tasks I had always done solo, like electrical repairs, painting the house, putting in a new deck, wallpapering, and so on. I don't think she ever wanted to walk on the roof as I removed leaves from the gutters, but I figured out that gardening together is fun. She has even surprised me when I ask her to get me a tissue or help me find a screwdriver, though sometimes I have to be careful not to make her feel I am ordering her around!

Let me stress that this is a delicate aspect of life to establish and live with on an ongoing basis. Telling is not asking; telling by its very nature can be regarded by the receiver as a command. Most of us – especially those who grew up in military families (like my wife) – don't like commands. One CEO we know actually jeopardized his new marriage when he made a list of what he expected his wife to do that week. Dumb. So, telling can get you into a lot of trouble. It might be necessary in emergencies, but there are probably few other times when it will serve you well. Asking – "Do you mind my asking you to" or "Honey, can you help me" work so much better.

Scenes from Our Relationship

❖ Being in business with my wife helped me learn how to ask for help. In our business, there were aspects I was good at, and there were aspects that she did so much better (and more profitably) than I could. Because we recognized that she was very good at things like marketing and facilitating interactions, we played to her strengths in these areas, and I recognized how much I needed her participation. Asking for her help became natural enough so that I could readily apply it to daily living. In turn, she recognizes my strengths and plays equally to asking for help base on these, as I do her. Here are some examples of things my wife and I have become comfortable at asking each other to help with.

Danny's List of Help from Her	Kathleen's List of Help from Me
Planning trips	Technology Issues (i.e. computer problems)
My clothing choices	Things that involve more physical strength
Finding friends	Getting to places on time
Things in his area of job expertise	Things in her area of job expertise

Editing my writing	Framing art projects
Making shopping lists	Driving directions
Planning money for retirement	Getting bills paid on time

Viva La Brain Difference

How often have you been confused by your partner's thinking? How will learning more about the differences in brain function help the two of you communicate?

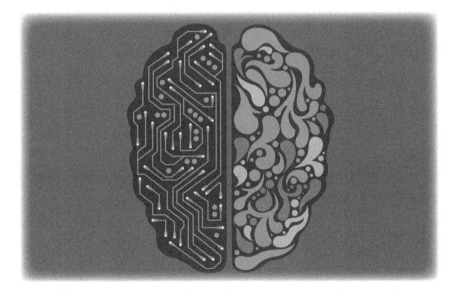

It's a generalization of course, but men have always thought that women have brains different from their own. It's just as true that men have different brains from other men! In general, both statements are kind of true, as shown in the book *Men Are from Mars, Women Are from Venus* (1992, Dr. John Gray). The truth is probably somewhere in between! It depends upon the particular brain. There are women with more masculine brains and men with more feminine brains. Knowing what kind of brain you and your partner each has is critical to engaging one another in your overall relationship. It helps enormously in dealing/processing with one another day after day. Here's some background:

Back in the 80s, Ned Hermann developed something called Whole Brain Theory, and a friend, Gene Myers, and colleague of mine was a leading practitioner. The theory proposed the idea that each person's brain has both dominant and subordinate ways of processing and acting on input from the environment and the people around us.

Some people respond linearly (step by step), while others respond holistically (taking the whole picture into account at once). Some people are predominantly creative; others, more detail oriented. Other characteristics fall, as these do, on a spectrum in which some are stronger than others in each individual. Whole Brain Theory refuted the notion that one way of thinking is superior to the other by describing the "sides" of the brain.

The brain's left hemisphere is the analytical region; the right hemisphere, the more creative part. I know that I'm a left-brain guy, who can plan and execute a wide range of needs very well. My wife, on the other hand, is very creative and a big-picture thinker. We realize that our varied strengths provide different (and more complex) approaches to our lives and to our life together. We realize that neither of us is thinking the "right" way and have recognized that we can use our differences to enhance the communication and needed solutions between us. This knowledge gives us the ability to minimize misunderstandings, to cooperate more easily, to work better together, and to fully enjoy our time with one another.

Reaching this stage took work, but it's work I recommend, because it can ultimately improve all your relationships. First, be aware that there are different brain dominances, and you can identify what yours is and what your partner's is. (Eventually, you may be able to identify any other person's, including your boss, coworkers, and/ or subordinates, where the skill could serve you well, too.) Help in figuring out brain dominance is available: There are tests and surveys online to make the process easier; some of the better known are Myers-Briggs and the Enneagram, but you can find others, as well. You can use any or all of them to get a clearer idea of how you and your partner are processing information and making decisions. Or you may be able to find a workshop offered in person to help you determine brain dominance.

Once the determination is made, you can begin the practice of using that information to interact with others – especially with your partner. Workshops are available both live and online to help with this, too, and you may be gratified to see how your communication and relationships improve. Let me tell you a workplace story that may help illustrate this. I once had a boss who was even more analytical than I am. He would explain a project to me in excruciating detail before I could begin work on it. I would sit there and listen but would never really "get" what was most important to him about the project. Once I knew how he processed things, I was able to ask him to diagram what he was saying, and it was from his visualizing the meaningful steps that I could tell what he needed me to do.

If you determine that you and your partner think alike, it can create harmony, but remember that harmony can also be created by voices singing different notes. My wife and I are aware that we respond differently to situations and needful decisions. We know that thinking about things in different ways is a strength in our relationship, just as it can be in yours.

Scenes from Our Relationship

❖ When my wife and I are making a decision, we each gather information in our own characteristic ways. We were recently deciding whether to buy a new car. I gathered technical information on the kinds of cars we might buy. I looked at price, gas mileage, horsepower, electric vs. gas, etc. My wife seemed to do none of these things. Instead, she read reviews, looked at pictures, and I swear she yawned when I talked about the details of how various cars performed. I felt like the Lone Ranger. But when we started to discuss a particular make or model, she knew its reputation and how it dealt with weather conditions like ours. I knew then that she wasn't ignoring me, just behaving according to the way she thought about stuff. When we chose a make and model, we did it together, having weighed different aspects and determined if the higher price was justified by the safety considerations. When we were deciding on a specific model, she surprised me by showing me that she had established the strengths of each model based on things we had never previously discussed, but which reflected each of our greatest concerns, including mine. I realized she had immersed herself in and integrated all the information available into an overall picture, while I was looking individually at each aspect separately. We work very well together – and so can you.

Praise Works

Everyone enjoys praise. Compliments make us feel better and motivated to do more—even when we look at what we are doing as drudgery. It can take some of us a concerted effort to give praise, but the rewards can be tremendous.

Husbands generally love to receive praise, but rarely give it in equal measure. That's a simple truth that needs changing. You can get some fantastic results if you learn how to give honest praise. I have learned that, in personal relationships, praise is the most effective way of reinforcing behaviors (I'm guessing you like to do things you know will earn you some praise; your partner will respond the same way).

In my work, I have studied a fair amount of practical human psychology, and as a business consultant and author of successful books on "The Language of Work Model," (Langdon, 1995, 2000, 2014, 2018) I've seen the effects of positive reinforcement on behavior in individuals and teams in companies, government, and nonprofits—and I know it works in personal relationships. Positive reactions in others are most successfully achieved in response to a reward (praise for people, which work like treats for animals). Whether I want my wife to cook my favorite meal or my dog to jump through a bicycle tire, I can more easily arrive at a solution I would like to see if I use a reward (praise for the wife; food and petting for the dog). Psychologists, like Dr. B.F. Skinner, have proven that telling us that we have done a good job benefits us all, whether the job was large or small.

In a partnership, praise can be a blessing. Whether your partner is running the home, raising children, caretaking aged parents, and/or working a full-time job, they have a lot of responsibility, and surely some of it can feel like drudgery. You benefit a lot from what your partner does, and I'm willing to bet that they (if they are a fulltime homemaker) don't have as much fun from day to day as you do. So if they are working hard at things you're happy not to be doing yourself—little, ordinary things—use praise liberally: "Thanks for making such a great pot roast," or "Thanks for taking the kids swimming today," or "Thanks for going to the ball game with me." or, "That's a great project result you achieved at work!" Your partner will appreciate hearing such things and think the more of you for having done so.

Praising your partner is one of the many ways you can show them how glad you are that they are your partner, that you do not think of them just as a housekeeper, or mother of your kids, or—as I like to say on occasion—my fishing buddy.

 ## Scenes from Our Relationship

❖ I recognized from the beginning that my wife is truly my partner, both at work and at home, and that sometimes her burden is greater than mine. She does so many things better than I do that it would be ridiculous for me not to acknowledge them by praising her. She is, for example, an accomplished artist—a talent she learned late in life near our retirement. I like seeing what she has produced and try to remember to compliment it for composition, and the like. She is a wonderful mentor to many women, and I am always fascinated how skilled she is at it and so I reinforce how grateful I am sure they are for her help. Praise is the lubricant by which we can make the skids of life easier—and it is free. I advise you to oil the cogs of your brain more to use praise more often.

❖ I do lots of projects around the house. I garden, rake, weed, and plant. I install water systems and redo the gravel parking area. I arrange for contractor's work—like a new front porch. I do things because of the sense of accomplishment they bring me personally, but also to contribute to our general well-being as a couple. I can honestly say that my wife almost always asks me, "Is your project finished? I want to come and see it!" She then praises me! When she finishes an art project, I try to return the favor by observing how skillful she has become in a certain technique or how expressive her artwork is. We have a mutual admiration society.

You Can't Change The Other Person

The only people who can change are people who change themselves. The idea that you can change someone else is an illusion.

*E*ver heard the saying "You are perfect. I love you. Now change"?
Not every husband or wife is wonderful. If you're in a relationship with a partner whom you were convinced you could change, you may be in for a big, awful surprise. We need to recognize that we all can be in denial about some characteristics of the other person when we were courting. We get so caught up in the feelings about them that we easily forget, forgive, or simply overlook existing negative attributes or behaviors. For example, we overlook or excuse their slovenliness, extravagant choices, prejudices and so on. We tell ourselves that will change after we marry. I have to tell you that's unlikely. Most of us are not specialists in human behavior, and we do not have the skills to help someone else change. No amount of complaining, consoling, berating, or even bribery will generally work.

It's likely that some changes will occur, to both of you, as you age, have children, lose jobs, face the deaths of friends or family, but there is no guarantee that those changes will be along the lines of what you've been hoping for. And even if they are changes you wanted, you are not the one making them happen. Outside forces are doing it, and in such a way that the change is self-driven.

The solution in this case needs to have happened before the relationship is made permanent. You have to pick carefully while you're dating. Notice if there are things you might want to change later—for example, if he or she dominates the conversation, or laughs loudly at things you don't find funny, or seems thoughtless. (By the way, be aware that good sex makes everything look rosier than it might actually be, so it may be wiser to postpone sex until the rest of the relationship is on steady ground—which men have a tougher time believing than women, generally.)

A person's personality is visible from the beginning if you pay attention, ask the right questions, probe for thoughts, feelings, and values. A friend of mine was dating someone whose sense of urgency was very different from his own. He would show up on time for every date. But she would not be ready—first, she would need to find her glasses, and then she wanted to change her coat. Once that was done, she would remember she hadn't fed the cat. They would finally leave 15-20 minutes later. Our friend loved (and loves) this woman, but he had to deal with boiling inside that she was never ready when he was. Instead of trying to change her, he decided she was like a cat, moving slowly from place to place, while he was more like a bird dog—all on point and raring to go. He decided that he would love her as she was, married her, and never criticized her.

If you are already in the relationship, accept that if something needs to be changed, you're better off making that change in yourself.

Scenes from Our Relationship

❖ I knew early on that my wife was not a meticulous housekeeper. She always has lots going on, and cleaning the house was never one of her priorities. (In fact, she is not even particularly neat.) On the other hand, I am both organized and tidy, and I don't mind doing my share of the chores. If I had thought while we were courting that she would change after our marriage, she would have been marrying a fool. At a party, I overheard her tell a friend, "I have a deep need for order—I just don't have any of the skills needed to achieve it." She is as accepting of my peccadilloes as I am of hers, and neither of us has ever asked each other to change. I have noticed, however, that over the years she is making more efforts to be tidy. She has chosen to change herself, and I hope I am doing the same thing for her.

❖ I am not great at change myself. In fact, I recently saw a bumper sticker that said, "Change is hard. You go first." One of my faults is that when I am shopping, I don't read labels carefully. I'll buy peppered salami when I wanted plain. Olives with pits when I wanted them pitted. The other day I thought I was buying corn bread mix at Trader Joe's, but when I got home and ready to use it, it turned out to be corn *cookie* mix. My wife knows that I will not readily change my ways, so she doesn't bother me much other to say, "Is this what you meant to buy?" "Did you happen to save the receipt for the corn cookies?" It's up to me then to correct the matter by taking the product back, exchange it, or enjoy the pepper on the salami. (I made the corn cookies, by the way. They are average! See Humor, Practice #3). I'm the one who has to change—no need to make her go first.

Be Honest:
Not Judgmental

Relationships are killed by lies. Even white lies have a way of being found out and getting caught in a lie creates chaos. Honesty is the best policy, even if it isn't easy.

onesty is the highest form of communication and a cornerstone of a truly functional relationship—one based on trust. And being totally honest makes, in my experience, a partnership grow and deepen, as long as a husband's "honesty" is not a way of criticizing his wife. Every one of us comes to a relationship with some secrets, and of course life itself can create many more. You might have some big secrets, but more often there are just little white lies here and there. Some of them may be based on dishonesty at work; others may relate to regrettable things said or done or actions mistreating others. (Serious infractions like fraud need to be dealt with in other ways, and I'm not referring to those here.)

The falsehoods that can create cracks or breaches in a relationship include such subjects as income, purchases, priorities, health, fidelity, work, goals, and values. All these areas—and more—depend on honest communication. Take an example from the workplace. I once worked for a company that needed to explore how ethics could be fostered in their environment, where bribes, kickbacks, and cronyism were all too possible. The executive who was tasked with encouraging the employees to be ethical in all their transactions told us that ethics was a simple concept, promoted by openness and honesty in all communications about everything. He pointed out that it's impossible to take ethical missteps in a work environment where everyone knows explicitly what everyone else's job is, what is allowed, and what isn't. (You might want to look at my guidance for clarity in the workplace, known as *The Language of Work Model.*)

The same is true in your personal relationship. The two of you must be completely honest without being afraid of having that honesty used against you, which means trusting that you will not be judged. Obviously, to maintain an honest and open relationship requires mutual desire for it. If your partner cannot be honest, it encourages you not to be honest either. And once you find dishonesty in your relationship, the two of you need to have a "come to Jesus" meeting, which can only succeed if it is mutual and effective. Under those circumstances, professional help may be needed, and that can be found in environments like a couple's retreat, a counseling group, or a 12-step program. If those are ignored or fail, the relationship can be in deep trouble. But if welcoming honesty into your relationship works, it can make your time together richer, deeper, and more rewarding.

Being honest demands several things: First, if you are trusted with your partner's secrets, you cannot share them with others. This could be hard for both of you—women because confidences shared with others may come more naturally to them and make it hard for them to censor themselves; men because by nature they dislike anything that makes them uncomfortable and they may tend to self-justify. Second, it is very important not to be judgmental. Your role is to listen and show empathy (see the next practice #13 in the book). You will want to encourage the honesty, not shut it down. Finally, their honesty is not yours to use against them any more than your honesty is theirs to use against you at some future time (also see practice #46, "Don't Live in the Past).

 **Scenes from Our Relationship**

❖ I suppose every person has a secret their partner doesn't know. One that surfaces within you and weighs on your conscience. That was true of me. The fact that I was keeping it from my partner bothered me a great deal. What it is, is frankly no one else's business nor would it matter to the point I'm making here, which is: Once I revealed this fact to my partner, she was able to help me process my feelings about it, accept its implications, and move on. I trusted her to do so because I know how she processes things (practice #14). What it did was banish my guilty conscience such that I don't think about it anymore. Importantly, I know that there is nothing between me and my relationship with her. That's a good thing, and I am all the better for it all.

❖ As a far less mysterious example of being honest with each other, my wife and I have been very open about spending money. We earn a comfortable living together, so there are extra resources for buying things and for travel. Still, we have an implicit agreement that when it comes to spending a large(ish) amount, there are no secret bank accounts, no hoarding money, and no significant purchases without prior discussion and agreement. This process implies full disclosure of not only finances, but how we process the other things that make up our life together: how we feel about everything, what we will and won't do, and the like. Always ask yourself, "Why keep secrets?" Secrets, when ultimately revealed, only diminish the trust you have in one another (unless, of course, you know how to process and move on). Not revealed, they only feel like heavy weights on your conscience.

Listen Well and with Empathy; Don't Offer Solutions

Gentlemen, it's not enough to just listen well (and many of us don't even do that). We must learn to listen without necessarily offering a "solution" to every issue. Successful relationships are based on expressing empathy for your partner's concerns and helping them work toward their own solutions.

This will be a two-fer practice, but related. It is **listening well** and its companion practice, **showing empathy**.

I am an action kind of guy who can get things done quickly and can usually show others what to do when asked. In the business world this may work well, since quick decisions sometimes must be made, and they are based on my recognized expertise in work organization and improvement. The problem is, as husbands, our wives are not always looking to us to tell them what *we* would do in the situation they have confronted and seek our counsel. By analogy, most are certainly not generally experts in human relations and partnership.

We need to realize that our partner is facing a challenge that they need to solve themself. (Reread that sentence with emphasis on the "they" and "solve themself.") The key notion in that sentence is THEY; not YOU! It's important to understand the difference. So, what do we—"Do it my way" kind of guys—do when asked for a solution? Gentlemen, I base my advice, when confronted with this conundrum, on my experience having done it wrong numerous times myself. The most helpful response will require some adjustment to your thinking and action, but I am confident you (as I eventually did) can handle it.

My wife taught me (and she was right!) that she is not telling me her problem in order for me to solve it. I don't think I ever realized that before! After I repeatedly made this mistake, she informed me—see the Coaching Practice #45—that she may not want my way of doing something; rather, she just wants me to empathize with her plight. She wants me to acknowledge/understand the challenge she is faced with. She wants validation that the way she feels about it is actually realistic and worth fretting about. Getting this validation immediately from me, the most other important person in her life, allows her to think more clearly so she can decide what she will do next. She will end up doing what she wants, the way she wants to do it. Do you get the difference, gentlemen? Here's the protocol:

First, listen well and offer empathy for whatever problem they are facing. For example, the problem might be that there is a computer glitch, or the sewing machine is stuck, or they can't find their keys. Tell them you understand their frustration, that you have faced it yourself and were similarly perplexed about how to solve it. "I am sorry you can't find the keys; that must be frustrating. I hate it when that happens to me." Or if it's a problem you haven't faced before, simply acknowledge that you see their frustration, and you are there to listen. "Wow, that sucks!" might be a sufficient response. This is the empathy step.

Second, after listening and providing empathy, you can ask if they considered a particular course of action (not saying what you personally did to solve that problem in the past). In the case of the lost keys: "Have you looked in such and such place?" or "When did you have the keys last?" might work, because those are *little* (unannoying/nonjudgmental) questions/cues that might help clarify things for them, leading them to a solution, but not telling them what you would do. Only then will they sense that you care and make a choice of action based on your hinted suggestion. You are treating your partner like an equal, not like a child or inferior who can't solve their own problems. Nirvana! (Important: if you really do know where the keys are, just tell them where you saw them. This is not a game.)

Scenes from Our Relationship

❖ My wife handles very complicated challenges in her personal and professional life. She provides sound suggestions and wise advice when friends need to think through handling a Covid-19 quarantine, or school issues for their kids, or caregiving challenges with an elderly relative. But when she is emotionally involved herself, she can, frankly, get a little squirrelly. She loses things in her art studio a lot—even things she just made or placed them "nearby." But recently she locked herself in the garage (admittedly because I did something different in securing the door to the garage), and I was miles from home. When she got in contact with me about her dilemma, I knew, upon talking to her on the phone, that I couldn't start with, "Well, what I would do is …." Instead, I told her it wasn't fair that the electricity went out and the garage door therefore would not open when she was still in the garage by herself and trying to get in the locked house. I could hear her calming down right then and there. Then she asked if she could open the door to the house with a credit card. "Nope," I said, "because it's a fire door." As we were talking, she remembered that the there is a latch you pull on a rope that releases the garage door. She opened the garage door and the problem was solved without my acting all superior with my own answer.

❖ My wife serves on the board of a nonprofit and, as part of a fundraiser, she typically sews about two dozen small purses. Later they are filled with goodies that make a very nice gift for women who appreciate fine craftsmanship. Now it is fairly routine that during the process of sewing she can make a mistake. She is a right brainer (see Practice #9), so this behavior is not surprising when details are involved. If she gets frustrated when this occurs, she tells me what the mistake is, and I know to listen with empathy and not offer any solution. Once she has expressed her frustration, she moves on to determining how to correct the error. By the way, offering solutions to problems that you know little about is not really a sound practice.

You Need to Be Able to Process Your Own S(tuff) First

The ability to process together whatever comes your way in this life you've chosen together will be key to its overall success. This begins with each individual's ability to process for themselves. Only then will you be able to process together.

was married before. So you might rightly question my expertise as a husband, but, unlike the proverbial old dog, I like to think that I learned some new tricks and was able to use what I learned the second time around.

Professionally, I am in the change business, so changing myself is something I can embrace (when nudged to see the light). (I should get my two wives together so they can compare notes to find out if I have improved or changed at all. I'd just as soon they only do so at my passing. I'll have you know they are friendly towards one another because of circumstances that are not part of this book. But I digress!)

I had at least two or three criteria when I considered getting married a second time. The first of these—and my wife-to-be and I discussed this when we were dating—was that my new mate had to have the ability to process her own stuff (although I used a four letter word also beginning with S). The reason I wanted this particular "transactional practice" was that I felt I was pretty good at processing stuff—whatever that stuff might be—and if I had a partner who could do the same, we would be, as they say, in "Hog Heaven!" Thus, if each of us was able to deal with our individual issues, then together we were likelier to solve the "peanut butter" (a phrase my wife likes to use) that comes along in all marriages. It turns out I was right about that, and I am passing that wisdom on to you (and your partner).

At its core, processing means that your partner is not your therapist, nor a target, nor your personal battering ram. It means that when something happens—and there is always something troubling in life--the person takes the "input" (another name for challenge, issue, difficulty, etc.) and does something (like thinking, praying, analyzing, coping, journaling, consulting experts, researching, etc.). That's the process. Then comes a conclusion, or result. Computers do this all the time, when it is called Input-Process-Output. Humans can do it as well. This, however, does not mean making job, living, and economic decisions by themselves. Instead, it means taking the drama and blame out of a situation when it's their own individual issue. Couples should always process their couple stuff together, but it begins first with us individually.

The notion of being able to process your own stuff, of course, applies equally to either of you in the partnership. You should be able to process your own issues to a fairly high degree before expecting to do so effectively with your mate. If you currently struggle with self-processing, I suggest you go learn how through resources like the one I will introduce shortly. There are penalties that come with failure to do so; your partner will constantly be running up against the brick wall that you present when the two of you discuss any contentious issue. If in the beginning you can't process well, you are really up against the even bigger wall of ever having a working relationship.

This notion of "processing your own (four-letter word beginning with S)" may seem like it would only apply to those who are currently dating, rather than those already married—but hold on. Recognizing that you may need help is an opportunity to fix what could be a central issue in your marriage. Since my wife came equipped to our marriage with that processing skill, I think how she came to be that way (since she wasn't born with it) is valuable to both men and women who not currently able to do so.

69

An Example of the Kind of Resources Available

By her own admission, my present wife came from a fairly dysfunctional family. She has siblings who might disagree, but it's part of their own history. Somewhere in her first marriage (yes, I am *her* second spouse, too) she discovered that she wanted to do a better job of solving issues for herself, for her then-partner (which proved impossible for many reasons), and especially for her children (which was possible). She was a professional trainer at that time and knew a thing or two about changing people, so she recognized that, while she had some processing skills, they needed honing. She joined a twelve-step program, even though she is not and never was an alcoholic. What she recognized was that she is the child of a parent who was. She started attending ACA (Adult Children of Alcoholics) meetings. I don't mean to suggest that everyone needs to get involved in a twelve-step program, but it is a good example of a resource for improving your ability to improve yourself and your relations with others, such as your partner.

I am sure there are other equally useful and available programs that help with processing skills. I believe that you will appreciate it once you have done it. I know from experience that your marriage can only benefit. I have a good male friend who confronted his need to improve his own processing of the stuff that was building a wall between him and his partner. He involved himself in an AA program, and it's been wonderful to note the difference it has made in his marriage. Self-assess, or ask a good friend, whether you can truly process things, and if not, get some help. Nobody else, other than your partner needs to know. And as a last caution, your partner should never become your therapist. It doesn't work!

Scenes from Our Relationship

❖ I am pretty good (but not perfect) at processing my own stuff, as needed. I came from a functional family, where self-reliance, problem-solving and working things out with others were encouraged. Thus, just as my wife learned how to process her own stuff as needed, I grew up seeing how it worked. Together we are able to deal well with the many things that have come up between us.

❖ Occasionally, especially when it comes to business matters, we do disagree on how to approach a project. This is to be expected in that we primarily operate individually and see things in different ways (see Practice #9, Viva La Brain Difference). I analyze any issue step by step and have a definitive plan for dealing with it. She, on the other hand, sees the broader picture from the outset. I would also instinctively tend to suggest to the client that "it" be done my way. This is largely because I am the originator of the process we use to solve business needs known as The Language of Work Model. However, I have learned to put my approach on hold while I think carefully about what my wife/business partner is pointing out about the client and the project and adjust my approach. I find the processing works all right if I also try doing it from her point of view. She does the same, and we "compromise" ways (see Practice #47, Accept Compromise) on what will work best for the client regardless of how we would individually do it ourselves. This collaboration uses the strengths of our individual process capabilities and works because we *are* processing individually first, and then collectively for the client. Using the same process for personal issues is an important aspect of how we broker partner relationship around all kinds of problems in our marriage.

On a very personal note, I had no idea what ACA was before I married my beloved wife, but I love that organization for what it did for her (as she has told me, and I believe her). You can research ACA and its mission yourself. What's critical here is that she felt she needed the help and got it (and occasionally she goes back to it and has even formed and facilitated similar groups for other women). What I learned from her is that it is the very process they follow that taught her to process her own stuff. I am so very thankful to them for doing so. I am very impressed by the initiative she took on to her own to improve her life. It contributes immensely to the ongoing richness of our partnership

Sorry: Doing vs Saying

It is hard enough for most men to say, "I'm sorry!" Some may think that sorry is just something they can show through actions. But that may not be enough.

*B*eing human, we are all bound to make mistakes. Some of us are prone to making many, and others fewer.

When you make a mistake, whatever it is, it's really best to admit, "I am sorry," vow to be better in the future, and mean it. Otherwise, if you can't confess, the agony of endless discussion (or unbroken silence) can consume both your will and your relationship.

The need to say you're sorry can result from any number of actions or inactions. You forgot to take out the trash, you forgot a time and place you were supposed to meet, you forgot to buy the milk during your errand to the grocery store, and on and on. Most times just acknowledging you forgot and doing some things to show you're sorry will be enough. But the really important times are when it's a big deal—e.g., you forget your anniversary or your partner's birthday, or you said something that hurt them, or numerous other egregious possibilities. Then not saying the words, "I am sorry" can be harmful.

If you find yourself in a situation where things seem to be falling into a downward spiral, and you know those words are just not going to come out of your mouth, AND you have been doing things to say you're sorry with no change, you might try asking what you can do to make your partner feel better . . . and you might get some cues. You can also suggest a treat or bring something home you know they like. By the way, I am not suggesting using roses or rings or even big purchases to fix things (although I know of a man who bought his wife a fur coat because he told a national industry newspaper that she was home recovering from a face lift! That might be terrible enough to require such a big gift.) Deciding to have a baby to fix a marriage is never a good idea . . . and if you have been unfaithful, better get marriage counseling and do a lot of interior landscaping if you want to keep them as your partner. For the big things, doing isn't enough, but many times, saying "I am sorry. How can I fix it?" will go a long way toward repairing the situation. But it needs to be said, in words, out loud.

Scenes from Our Relationship (a Wife's Take)

❖ There is a man's view of sorry, and then there is a woman's view. So, when I was writing this, I asked my wife for her input on what convinces her that I'm really sorry. Here is what she said: "It is my observation that many men have trouble saying those precious words, 'I'm sorry.' Instead, they do things that, as wives, we have to understand are the apology. For example, after a little tiff over something very tiny, but which disappointed me, I will realize that all of a sudden, my (very discreet) 'honey-do list' is being taken care of. He hasn't told me he is sorry; he hasn't told me that I was right about whatever we were discussing—no, he doesn't come to me the way a woman might and say, 'Can we talk about that? I was wrong; I know I hurt your feelings; I want to know what you are thinking and how I can be better.' No, I don't think guys are constructed that way!

So, rather than want my very masculine husband to act in a very feminine way, I opened my eyes to what was occurring after one of these tiffs that every couple has. Suddenly he would ask if I wanted to catch a particular movie before it left town. Or he would ask me where I wanted some hooks put up. Or I would find him outside, pruning a tree I had been remarking needed help. He was DOING 'I'm sorry,' not saying it."

❖ For my part (Danny writing), it has taken me a number of years to simply get the words, "I am sorry for …." whatever it is out of my mouth. Like most people, I seemed to find it more desirable to dance around and around about an issue rather than justly simply come out with the words. So, I decided a few years ago to change my behavior on this front. After a few times of being able to say I am sorry, I discovered that the issue(s) at hand resolved itself much quicker and I was no less of a person for having done so. I recommend trying it. You'll be surprised.

Acknowledge Moody Times

Everyone has moods, and now and then one of them is crotchety. How do you help your partner distinguish between your just being "in a mood" and your being in a mood that they caused?

*A*lthough I try to portray a positive attitude toward life, there are times when I can become cranky. It happened most vividly early in my married life when I was trying to fix our used washing machine for the first time. Some part had just worn out, and while I knew what the part was, I could not immediately get and fix the washer, because the part would take a couple of weeks (no Amazon then) to arrive by mail. That time lapse made me cranky! I wanted it fixed now!

These days, when I am in a cranky mood, I have learned to tell my wife, "The washing machine is broken!" She understands that says, "I am trying to get something done and have little patience with the way it's going." It could be something as little as not having a return receipt in hand or as large as the car having an intermittent problem. She immediately knows that I am indicating my state of mind. I am telling her that something in my life is broken, and I'll be a bit moody until I get it resolved. She knows that I am telling her my moodiness does not mean that I think she is doing anything wrong. I may even need and request her help; I want her to bear with my attitude and not blame herself for it.

Stating clear messages is vital in any interpersonal transaction, but especially with your partner. Otherwise your partner may not know why you are moody and think perhaps it is something they did. Moodiness can build up over time, and then the relationship can be in deeper trouble. It may even generate arguments if left unchecked (frankly, I do not like arguments). So, I have learned that it is better to "name that moody tune" and be aware of what's playing in the background. Your partner should really appreciate knowing and can then allow you the time to get over it without believing you are upset at them.

In order to tell your partner your state of mind, you need to have recognized that you have an issue with something. Your partner may give you cues to help you. My wife is pretty good at reading my face (practice #34, Nonverbals). She can see that I am puzzled or worried about something, so she simply says so in a nonthreatening way: "You have a puzzled look on your face. What are you thinking about?" I often go deep inside myself to consider a problem, rolling it around and around in my brain, and do not realize it is affecting my behavior. While I'd like to recognize my issues on my own (and often I can), I don't mind my partner helping me see the light. Self-reflection and acknowledgement go a long way when it comes to why you are moody and letting others know.

Scenes from Our Relationship

❖ Recently, we were traveling in New Zealand. I discovered that I had made a mistake that meant either we needed to change a flight, or we needed to change our B and B reservation to stay an extra night. Since I like to fix things immediately, I told her the washing machine was broken and we needed to get to the airport and fix our flight and rental car arrangements, and we had to do it at once. She had her own priorities for the morning, but when she heard the code ("the washing machine is broken") she understood I was going to be cranky until I solved the problem. She didn't argue with me; she immediately got into the car, and off we went to the airport. We fixed the flight date and car rental together in half an hour and moved on in our journey no worse for wear. My familiar practice of clearly communicating my distress made it all work out well. Then we could go on the things she wanted to do that morning.

My advice would be that you and your partner just learn to name an issue for what it is, deal with it, and move on. You will both find you can be much the happier if you do.

Additional Note

Oh, and while I'm on the topic of fixing things, let me strongly suggest that you make it a practice not to procrastinate. Men who get in the habit of doing things only on their own schedule are traveling in dangerous territory, where nagging may be crouching behind every little or big project. My wife tells a story from her first marriage about a hole in the ceiling that was there for 18 months before her significant other got around to it. That's asking for trouble. If nothing else, establish a timeline for repairs, buying things, and the like, and stick to it as a demonstration that you care about the space you share. There are, after all, two or more of you who will be affected by your thoughtfulness.

Recognize that Your Partner Has a Life of Their Own

It makes a huge difference in your relationship when you recognize that your partner has talents, different from your own, that they might like to develop and use. Notice them and ask yourself how you can support and encourage them.

omen, it seems, are more social beings than their partners. They seek out others with like minds, get together often, commiserate about all kinds of things, and often talk about you, their children, others' children, other women, or whatever comes to mind (it can also be business, politics, entertainment, cooking—the list is endless). They cherish interaction as a form of making love visible in the world. One saying about this is that "women tend and befriend." They seek out social, professional, and volunteer group activities, often with other women. And today large numbers of professional/working women have lives outside the home.

Your partner may want you to join them for some of the activities that matter to them, whether you care to or not. If you choose to participate in their life at times, it will help if you find ways to enjoy that participation, largely because you shouldn't try to always decline; you may want to show your partner you know how important the activities are to them. (That old adage, "If you can't lick 'em, join 'em!" applies). Consider the possibilities of what might happen if you choose *not* to participate in activities, they ask of you. We know of at least one marriage that failed (in part) when one person wanted to learn to dance, and the other refused!

I recognized long ago that my wife has a life of her own. She has needs that I realize she must meet in order to fulfill herself. She is often interested in the content of an activity, but sometimes she wants to connect with people she knows or will meet. Some of these occasions are easier for her if I participate, because of mutual friends or interests, distance, time of day, road conditions, or because she wants to hear my insights and reactions. There are other times she does not really need me to participate. You see, at times, it's about her needs, not mine. I try to recognize the difference. If she asks, I go. If she doesn't ask, I find other things to do. And it really won't hurt me to go with her, because if she's asking me, that's another of her needs, and I can fulfill that one easily. I may have learned this growing up since my mother did scads of things for self-fulfillment, out of a driving desire to help others, and to meet her social needs. Part of this was since she was a "single mom," but mostly she had a life that she wanted to fulfill in all kinds of ways. Even if you did not have that experience as a role model of a female, you need to realize that your choosing to support your partner's activities enriches her life. And you might also recognize that such activity is good not only for them, but for *you* as well. I am a willing partner in my wife's self-fulfillment, and it goes without saying, that she is a willing participant in what I like to do (e.g., occasionally attend a ballgame with friends). Who would not want mutual fulfillment to be the outcome of a partnership?

Scenes from Our Relationship

❖ My wife is an active person. Besides her professional career, she belongs to a few social groups (church, art, book club, women's discussion groups, etc.), organizes and facilitates events for others, believes in and practices social justice, serves on the boards of a nonprofit and a university academic program, and in general has a wide range of friends and acquaintances—much more than I do. For some of these activities, she likes my "accompanier" participation, and others she does not. I have, however, the option of participating. Additionally, she has at least one activity that I really wish she didn't have (volunteering in our homeowners' association), but I wouldn't try to stop her. Indeed, I support her by listening to all the dysfunctional interactions she faces with that group when she needs me to listen.

❖ Although at first I worried it would be a struggle for me to participate in some of her activities, I decided to try some of them just to see what would happen. I can say, almost universally, that I ended up, much to my surprise, enjoying these encounters, largely because there is frequently someone new to meet and chat with. Often the experience itself has an enjoyable interactive element, or I learn something new. I call it my "keeping an open mind!" Whether it is a political protest, an art walk, poverty simulation, or a speaker at a local old theatre, I often have to convince myself to go and participate, and I know I would lose out by saying, "No, it's not my kind of thing," even if I thought it was. I recommend that, if you are not currently doing it, you give it a try.

There is Nobody Better
To Spend Time With

Who would you really rather be with through life's adventure? If not them, then whom? If the answer is yourself or someone other than your partner, you need to reassess your priorities.

Males seem to like being with other guys! This liking ranges from some of the guys to a whole lot of the guys. The guys from work, the sports team friends, the old high school or college gang are all temptations. A lot of time can be spent as spectators, playing some pick-up basketball at the gym, fishing, a few hundred rounds of golf, or drinks at a local pub. That is somewhat well and good, but what about spending equal or even more quality time with your wife?

Is it possible that your time with the boys is excessive? Who's your best friend anyhow? And if it's not your spouse, then why not? They are the person you have sex with, eat with, perhaps raise kids with, argue, socialize, and live with. If there is really anyone else you would rather spend the bulk of your time with, then I suggest you may have a fundamental relationship issue and may want to get some professional help. Or you can just take it upon yourself to make some adjustments. You may want to remember that you're a husband first, not primarily someone else's fishing buddy!

I really like being with my wife. I hold her hand and process things with her. We worked together professionally in our consulting practice (although I am not suggesting everyone should or even could do that). We are often with mutual friends, travel extensively, attend social events (some of which I can't say I am that crazy about; see practice #17), and so on. We do have things we each like to do on our own. There is a workable balance that accommodates us both.

It's important to watch for an imbalance that leans too heavily on being with the boys. Ask yourself how much time with the guys is enough—and how much of your time does your wife need? For a rich, fruitful partnership, don't make your partner compete with the guys! And here's one reason why:

Many, if not most, partners seem to want a soul mate.* That may sound corny to men, but even if you have never considered it before, it could make you happier as well. According to Merriam Webster, the definition of a soul mate is (1) a person who is perfectly suited to another in temperament; and (2) a person who strongly resembles another in attitudes or beliefs. Those definitions describe two people who connect with each other intimately and deeply. My own definition of soul mate would be that she is the one I'd most like to be with, to do loads of things with, the person I most love.

I know, I know. Some of you might say, "My partner doesn't want to spend that much time with me!" If that's the case, you can try to make time with you more to their liking—for example, less beer and more roses. Really listen to what they are telling you, and don't react by mocking or belittling them. Start sharing more of the little things that make up your life when you are not with your partner—the bird you saw on your way to work, the sunset on your way home. Just little observations, little ways to increase your connection to your partner, little moments of sharing your inner life with them.

Scenes from Our Relationship

❖ Even though she really is my soul mate, I can sometimes forget my wife is separate from me. While I do not have much need for other people to understand who and what I am, my partner needs it from me. So, I work at being sure she knows how special she is to me. We take a daily walk together, and I already mentioned spending early morning time together (see #4, Start The Day Together). But last summer we added something friends who have been married for 60 years have been doing. Two or three times a week we have a beer or a cup of tea together, accompanied by casual chat, but not trying to solve major problems in the world. Much of this is done after dinner where we sit on the back deck and chat as the sun sets; sometimes under warm blankets when it is cold out. In any or all our activities, I make sure she always knows that she's the one I want to spend my time with—not puttering around the house nor hanging with the guys. I have plenty of time for those things, but I always want to be sure there are incredibly special times for us!

*I want to say something about having a soul mate:

Since the term "soul mate" is such an often-used, but not well understood or agreed upon way to refer to your partner, I'd like to give you even more of my take on it than I gave you with my definition, above. It's not really something you start a relationship with—it is what develops between the two of you (if you are really lucky) over time. But you must work at it!

I know Kathleen is my soul mate because we connect in so many ways, while at the same time we seem to be so different. Our connection is based on a deep-seated understanding that comes from having interacted so many, many times; we always come away with a new understanding, as well as a resolution of whatever it is that distressed either one of us. Partnership is fraught with things that go wrong, influences from other people, and much of it can simply be out of our control. To know that you live day after day with a special person who assures that we will survive (and have loads of fun together), is what makes for my picture and warm feeling of a soul mate. For this and many other reasons, there is nobody I would rather spend time with!

Avoid Nit-Picking

Just as praise creates rewards (see practice #10) in a relationship, nitpicking creates harm. Correcting and criticizing your partner wears them down. You can learn not to do it—in public or at home.

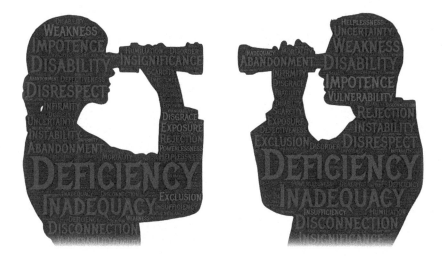

A couple's life is filled with opportunities for one of them to dislike what the other one is doing or saying. These kinds of annoyances are magnified by kids, because kids are constantly learning and need your input (even if they think they don't). Reminding children of manners or rules can become habitual and can carry over easily to how we treat each other as partners. There are always some occasions in which adults act like children, of course, and that makes it even easier to fall into treating them like that.

But how you live your life together as a couple, aside from kids (if that were possible), is an important discussion for every partnership to have. That discussion applies to major things like whether both of you will work; if so, whose job will take precedence if you need to move or in emergencies that will arise; where you will live; whether children are in the picture; and so on. Those things are not what nitpicking is about, because they aren't nits. Nitpicking happens when it's part of the little things that make up daily living. It's usually easy to identify what bugs you about your partner (and what is bugging them about you). For the harmony of the relationship, nagging or one-upping is not going to change the behavior. It's just going to keep hurting.

Some common places where nitpicking can occur:

While Shopping Together

My wife buys based on price, and I buy based on quality. Other couples may have other preferences. Anytime there is even minor disagreement, there is potential for lecturing or arguing. We try to make a practice of each of us offering one alternative or suggestion and sometimes the one who offers first gets to make the choice. For instance, if I choose Jif Creamy peanut butter and she suggests the store brand, which costs less, if I say, "I like this brand better," the decision is made, and we move on. Sometimes it makes no difference. A generic over-the-counter medication is just as good as the brand name, for example.

Social Settings

Your partner is telling a story during dinner or drinks with friends. They say it happened six months ago, but you know it was eight months ago. You're tempted to correct them—but really, who cares? Before you speak, ask yourself why it matters and let it go. At a restaurant it is particularly important to avoid correcting each other, complaining, or disagreeing over very minor matters like salad choice or having dessert. Making an issue of such unimportant things as whether their napkin is in the wrong place, or they are using their knife as a fork are often not that really important in the scheme of things. It's better just not to nitpick about any of that. If it really distresses you, you can ask your partner about it when you get home. Remember, each person has to want to change themselves (practice # 11).

At Home

We make a rule to try to be positive even when we're asking about something that happened outside. Using the above example, I would say, "It made me a little uncomfortable when you used your napkin as a pointer at dinner. Would you be able to not do that when we're out?" We both try to ask for what we would like and see what happens. If the answer is no, it's best to just let it go and live with it.

 Scenes from Our Relationship

❖ For a number of years, my wife and I were constantly reminding one another (a form of nitpicking) that one of us had left the heated-toilet seat up (I wonder which one of us was doing it!). Eventually, this periodic reminding became an irritant to both of us, so we stopped talking about it and just each put the seat down anytime we saw it was up. It was as if we finally recognized that it wasn't that big a deal, and it was much more rewarding to not bug each other and simply be happy.

❖ I once knew a husband who, every time a disagreement came up, spouted a list of egregious things he felt his wife had done in the past. Many of these were not necessarily related to the disagreement at hand, but he felt compelled to let his partner know how imperfect he thought she was. The marriage didn't survive when she grew tired of his living in his past.

What Can You Be Relied On To Do?

A great partnership is about what you share. But you don't have to share all the jobs. Things run smoothly when there are tasks each of you can be counted on to do regularly, eliminating the angst of who was supposed to do what.

I never assume that anything is exclusively "women's work," and my wife does not assume certain things are only "man's work." We each have our individual strengths, and we use them to the best advantage for our relationship. Our agreement on who best handles what makes our home run dependably and lovingly, as a true partnership. This means setting up a routine, and sticking to it, involving the day-in, day-out ordinariness of life: the cooking, the cleaning, the shopping, picking up kids, taking parents to the doctor, washing the dog.

Sometimes there will be reasons you have to pinch-hit for your partner, and vice versa, but in normal circumstances, go with your strengths. We had a colleague whose home had not established the routine. It became apparent after he died that she had been unquestioningly relying on him to do a whole lot of things he had not been doing: clearing old newspapers and magazines out of his office, organizing finances, and strategizing about their retirement savings (of which there turned out to be none). Her situation made me wish he had read (and followed) this book well before his death, so that part of his very real love for her would have helped him plan some routines. (Fortunately, his wife was a talented and energetic woman who was able to take care of the issues she faced when he was gone.) I am guessing her attitude towards him was little different once he was gone.

A husband should have a routine that his partner can depend on, and as a couple, they can see that it covers the needs in the relationship. Outside help—for instance, a gardener—can be plugged in if neither of you has the time or the ability to handle something, but that becomes part of the expectations for the smooth running of the partnership.

Scenes from Our Relationship

❖ My wife knows she can count on me to take out the garbage. She is certainly capable of doing it herself (and if I'm traveling or otherwise tied up, she does), but she knows it's an accountability I have assigned to myself. She also counts on me to buy the groceries (and I like doing so), and to assure that there is gas in the car. I also get the cash from the ATM, and I pay the bills. I do the barbecuing and gardening, but she builds the meals around what I cook and harvest. She ensures that the bathrooms are clean and sweet-smelling, keeps track of movies and TV we might like, and finds the bargains when we need things for the house. She is also in charge of our social lives. I write, she edits what I write. I scheme, and she supports my schemes, but also contributes her innate creativity to our activities and our lives. She is free to do so because she knows I will take care of the activities I have committed to (as does she). It is part of our foundation for a bump-free partnership—and it works.

❖ I refer to myself as her ATM – Any Time Man. Thus, when she needs things, she can always call on me. As much as it might seem primarily for things out of the ordinary, I consider this part of my routine. It's my way of being reliable. Ready to stand up and serve what needs to be done—big or little. Rather than having a state of mind that says, "I should really not bother him with my needs!" it rather let's her know that I can be counted upon. I feel the same about her.

Flowers Now and Then

Nothing lights up your partner more than flowers. (Well, maybe diamonds, but those are not for day to day.) A great husband will bring flowers as a little reminder that his wife is cared for and loved.

I haven't always been a romantic. Then I discovered that there were a lot of rewards to being romantic. Wives (note: same sex partners decide for yourselves) in general love romantic gestures, because those gestures liberate them from daily routines like changing diapers, being caretaker for parents or kids, dealing with teenagers, what's going at their job, running errands—and at the same time, a romantic gesture can make your wife remember back to when your life together was new. That was a heady time, when you couldn't stop thinking about each other with eagerness, even with hunger. Now, perhaps many years or even decades later, that time can be brought back into your lives with a small investment at a grocery store or a florist. By the way, while a small bouquet does wonders, a larger bouquet is a diamond!

Flowers say, "I thought about you today." When they see the flowers in a vase on a table or sideboard, they are reminded that you really did think about them—and that you might be doing it on days you don't bring flowers home. Jewish men may make a practice of bringing a bouquet on Fridays to put on the Sabbath dinner table, which is a great custom, but I'm suggesting you do it on days that do not mark occasions like the Sabbath, their birthday, or Valentine's day. Flowers appearing at odd times show that you can think of them when not asked to do so by advertising, that you can give them when it's not an obligation or expectation.

The key there is "odd" times; if you regularly present flowers to her on the first of every month, it becomes routine, and its surprise value can wane. Flowers brighten up a room and a home, and your partner may get a boost from being able to boast to friends and guests that her husband "just gave me that beautiful bouquet for no reason at all." By the way, wildflowers have generally the same effect.

Scenes from Our Relationship

❖ My stepdaughter, seeing a lovely flower arrangement I had given her mother, asked, "Does Danny bring you flowers every day?" My wife told me how much she enjoyed knowing that her daughter had seen clearly how much I cared for her mother.

❖ Another time, my wife and I drove into a city near us where she had an all-day meeting to attend. I went along so that we could do something together once her meeting was over, and while she was tied up, I explored the city on foot. I ended up at a Saturday farmer's market, where I bought her a rather large bouquet of bright red gerbera daisies, which I had delivered to her meeting room. She was delighted (and a little embarrassed) by this show of love, and her colleagues were charmed by the gesture. Of course, they asked if it was her birthday, and when it became obvious it was a spontaneous display of affection, everyone grinned—and I'll bet some other women envied her!

We'll Never Run Out of Things To Talk About

Conversation helps make a good relationship better, and in a great relationship, you never run out of things to talk about. It's easy.

The other day my wife and I were having dinner at a lovely restaurant with fine food. Next to us was a table at which three of the four people (in their 30s) were silently looking at their individual cell phones; the fourth was talking on her phone to someone as she ate. They represented two couples who might have just as well all been eating alone. I don't think there is anything sadder than a couple (or two) at a restaurant not conversing with one another. They might as well not be at the same table. If they interact at all, it is simply to say, "Pass the salt" or "This meat is tough."

Today's social media can substitute time with one another (and with children and friends). It seems as if the art of conversation has been lost, and it is hardest on a partnership that falls prey to it. Most healthy relationships must not allow this to happen. And there is an easy solution: You can put your phone down (better yet, turn it off) and invest in real, one-on-one (or more in social settings) conversation.

If you believe you are not a good conversationalist, welcome to the world I used to inhabit. You see, I grew up as a pretty shy person. I hardly said a word, and my brothers and sisters often observed, "Danny hasn't much to say. He's a quiet kid!" I realized that I was and wondered for years whether this was who I am or was there anything I could do about it. It wasn't until my first year in college, living with so many others, that I figured out the answer: People like to talk about themselves. Therefore, if I just asked a question about them, they would answer. After that first question, I could ask another. Or they would then ask me a question about me, and I would answer it, which meant I was talking. I could also comment on something they had said. Next thing you knew, we were having a real conversation. It didn't matter where I was—in a crowd, in a bar, at the store, in church, or just walking down the street. For example, my wife and I were recently with some new friends from Europe, and I saw that he had mastered the same technique of asking questions. When there was a lull in the conversation, he asked what kind of food we liked best. Did we cook together? Were there good restaurants in our hometown? He kept the conversation going the same way I had learned to do! You can as well!

The rewards of conversation are many. For example, once in Peru I asked a question of a couple as we crossed a life-threating busy street together. From that question we got invited to their house, to a reception at a restaurant they owned, and even to their grandson's wedding. A client recently observed, "Danny doesn't say very much, but when he does it's either funny or really profound." I guess I'm still not really talkative but practicing asking questions has made me more comfortable altogether–and allowed the real me (humorous and deep) to come out. And if conversation with relative strangers can result in so many good things, imagine how much richer conversation with your partner can be.

Scenes from Our Relationship

❖ Since I wasn't always a great conversationalist, I distinctly remember, when we first started dating, observing to my wife-to-be how it might be difficult for us to always have things to talk about. She mused for a minute over that and responded wisely that we needn't worry, but I still kind of did. Thankfully, I've learned that she was right—it has not been a problem. I really enjoy talking to her. I see her as a fount of knowledge, experience, and (if all else fails) of excellent guesses—that is, she will provide a very likely answer, but sometimes add that she does not know for sure. (It turns out she is right a very high percentage of the time.) She often says to people that she runs "1-800-opinion" on any subject at all. So, when we are out to lunch, I just start asking questions. "What are you reading?" "What's that book about?" "Did you ever go camping when you were growing up?" "Did you and your family see anything interesting on road trips?" I can go on and on, and my partner is fully capable of both responding and asking me questions in return. I like to talk now. It makes our relationship beautifully vibrant.

❖ My wife has assured me, further, that a little quietness between us occasionally is really all right. Again, she knew of what she spoke. I have learned from her that, when you really like someone, you will never run out of things to talk about. I've learned that there are easy techniques to ensure and enhance conversation with your spouse--or anyone else, for that matter. And, I also learned that when you have good practices, such as those given in this book, you and your partner will always be comfortable with one another, both talking and in silence. If I had a motto for such, it would be, "Talking Is Liberating."

Acknowledge Your Partner's Opinion

Your partner is as important as you are. Even if you disagree, acknowledge their opinions.

$\mathcal{S}$ome couples act as if any difference of opinion must be resolved by one person being "right": "You are the winner, yessiree!" There are better ways to engage in nurturing a relationship, because if there is a winner, there must be a loser, and neither of you wants to be that.

There are numerous ways in which you can support your partner without necessarily saying you always agree with them. For instance, they may have strong political feelings that run contrary to your own. Rather than put those feelings down by your disagreement, acknowledge their right to have an opinion and then give your own as a fact, not in order to try to make them change their mind. The same goes for what movies to go to, what to spend money on, where to go on vacation, what to have for dinner—all the small and larger issues that life together presents.

You can go through life bickering, if you both enjoy it, but I advise against doing it in public. Most of us have lots of opinions and often we state them in front of others. But no one wants to be known as stubborn, mean, or the butt of a joke. You have some choices to make as a couple: What's really important, what's somewhat important, and what really doesn't make a damn bit of difference in the big picture. Agree on those things, and you can agree how and where you will disagree.

Acknowledging your partner (or your) opinions does not mean rolling over, conceding to their way of thinking, indulging their every whim. It just means that you will be respectful of their opinions, rather than dismiss them, joke about them, or use them to put them down. A partnership is a great opportunity for both of you to become more than either of you is alone. And respect, coupled with quiet listening and acknowledgment, create a chance for opinions to change—their own, or even yours.

Scenes from Our Relationship

❖ When my wife and I disagree on something factual, she generally handles it by looking up the answer. For example, if I say John Kennedy was elected president in 1961, and she is sure it was 1965 (and if it's important to us, for some reason), we check it on Google or ask someone else if we're at a party—fact learned, problem solved, move on. In many cases we have matured enough in our relationship to understand that a lot of things (i.e. the precise year Kennedy was elected) don't really matter, and that we can discuss the things that do (i.e. I was in the Peace Corps and she was at college at that time) without fighting about what isn't all that important in the grand scheme of things. In the short form, before you correct someone over a minor point, decide just how important it is to do so! If it isn't important, drop it.

❖ When our very old furnace needed replacing, my wife had this notion that we should have a heat pump, given that our propane gas bill for heating was very high. I resisted the idea, not with a loud "No Way!" but rather with a fair bit of foot dragging. As I look back, I can't really recall what I might have been objecting to. Eventually, we both investigated the reasons for adding a heat pump, and I talked to neighbors who loved theirs. Together, we decided on a heat pump. It turns out it wasn't so much about the device itself as it was about spending the money to purchase one—they are expensive. (I also have to admit that it hadn't been my idea, and I think of the house sometimes as my area of expertise. I needed to do a little processing (see practice #14) myself. What a fool I was since, as it turns out, it has saved us lots of money and will pay for itself in a few years. And it has several other benefits in terms of including air conditioning, an air filter for mitigating allergies, etc. I certainly support her decision (opinion) now, and I tell her how brilliant she was to have it.

A Little Publicity In Your Marriage!

Let the world know that you are crazy about your partner—that's a great reflection of your relationship. It can be very easy to be complacent and assume everyone knows your love story. But it can mean the world to your partner when you let the world in on how you feel.

Was once involved in a spiritual study group that was composed of 8 women and me. Without being overly boastful about it, I let the group know (during initial introductions) how much I loved my wife (who by the way, in one of her many community activities, had organized these study groups for several years). During the 30 weeks that the group met once a week, naturally we grew close as a group, and each of the women remarked that seeing how much I loved my wife encouraged them to increasingly express their love to their partner. I think many marriages were enhanced that year. The ability to focus on the love we have for our spouses led to added appreciation for each other.

It turns out that there are numerous opportunities to let others know how we feel about our partner. A simple one that I often take the opportunity to do is when introducing one another to a new group: "This is Kathleen, my very significant other" is one way I do this. Another is to hold her hand in almost any public setting, and still another is telling our granddaughter that I love her grandmother very much. I express my joy in traveling with my wife during casual conversations about a region of the world we have been to when we are in social settings. Certainly, our experiences in working professionally together over many years is something to brag about. This in particular seems to impress others who then remark that they could never work with their spouse.

Compare this to the temptation to complain about our partner's behavior—in this case, in front of them. One guy we know, but hadn't seen for a long time, decided to tell us how much his wife liked to bitch—when he could have mentioned how pleased he was that she appreciated the time he spent organizing the garage. Or when he brought home great fish from his trips with his buddies.

The put-down stopped all conversation—how can you ask a leading question after that complaint? And she was absolutely mortified, although she tried to laugh it off.

Since there are all kinds of occasions for expressing to others how you feel about your partner, you can make sure they feel treasured. You only need to notice such opportunities and commit to telling the world in a positive way how you feel. It will strengthen your relationship, for sure.

 ## Scenes from Our Relationship

❖ A few months ago, my wife and I were at the audiologist's office for my wife's first visit to check out the need for hearing aids (she likes to refer to them as "ear jewelry"). This audiologist has an interesting practice on the first visit of asking the patient's spouse to fill out a form describing their own experience with their partner's hearing. I guess this is because the spouse is the person who spends the most time with their partner and can capture how the hearing loss affects them, as well as others. *Pretty smart of that audiologist*, I thought to myself. So, I dutifully filled out the two-page form, noting at the end, "I love my wife!" A month or so later, on a follow-up visit during which I also accompanied my wife, the receptionist remembered me and my wife, specifically because of my "love" note on the form. She was apparently deeply touched that I had noted my love for her and said so to my wife. Finding little ways, especially if you have been together for a long time, to let the world know how much you love your partner will make them feel wonderful and pay dividends for you. When your partner feels wonderful, so will you!

❖ As I have mentioned elsewhere, my wife and I were in business together for 25 years. We had a consulting practice based on a business model I had originated in the early '90s. We often did work with major enterprises helping them to reorganize, institute cultural change, introduce new technology, and improve processes and jobs. In describing our work to others, often in social settings where such things come up, I almost always note that my partner/wife is a master facilitator. That is easy to do since she really is. It isn't hard to see the positive reaction (i.e., smiles) of people, as well as my wife's smile. The business was not just about me and my model. It was highly successful because of what she brought to it, in implementing the model and facilitating discussions with clients. They were so impressed at how much she came to know about their business and could talk about in their terms. I was too!

Your Appearance:
Listen to Your Partner

A second opinion about the way we look is very beneficial. Dress and general appearance are most often event-driven, so ask your partner's opinion before you both walk out the door. You never know—your fly might be open!

I am like many men, I think, in that I like to wear what *feels* comfortable. Some women, I have found, feel the same way. But many women, my wife included (and perhaps yours, too), want us to wear what *looks* good and makes them feel good, especially in social situations. There can be a great difference between what feels comfortable and what looks good. I am comfortable in blue jeans and a t-shirt, but my wife tells me I look great in a tux (or dress shirt, sweater, etc.).

A wonderful friend of ours told me once that she observed that wherever we go, I usually wear a t-shirt and jeans, and my wife is "dressed well." I am not sure I ever noticed myself that much—the jeans are clean, and I don't smell. Her comment, however, led me to realize that I am pretty casual, while my wife is stunning. I started to think I could do better both for myself and in relation to my partner. You might want to think about the impression you make when the two of you go somewhere.

I do like to be comfortable, but I don't want to be thought a slob! The trouble is, I don't necessarily recognize when I border on being underdressed for a given situation. We go out often… to a movie, to dinner, for a trip to the mall, or on other, more formal occasions such as weddings, funerals, or business meetings. So, I have made it a practice to ask my partner in advance what she thinks the dress code is. I will also ask how I look before it's too late to make a change.

I have learned to take suggestions on my dress code so that I can be sensitive to my partner's often unspoken desire for me to look good. She is careful about criticizing others and doesn't want me to feel bad, so she generally does not comment on my dress unless I ask. So, it's up to me to ask whether, given the situation, if I do in fact look appropriate for the occasion. When I ask, I know she appreciates my recognizing her impeccable sense of what's suitable.

If you experience the same lack of judgment about proper clothing that I do, here are some guidelines to help. Ask about your dress code when you and your partner are going to a shared experience where people may judge you not as an individual, but as a couple. For example, if she is in a dress and you are in jeans—that may make people think you are mismatched. If you're at a funeral where she's wearing black, and you have your favorite loud shirt on, the "Fashion Police" would give you a ticket, perhaps embarrassing her. The easiest way to know if your partner thinks you are all set is to ask while you are dressing, not on your way out the door. If they are sensitive to this, they will ask you about their own look, "How does this scarf look with this blouse?" Nothing wrong with dressing one another, so to speak!

(Oh, by the way, never dress in matching outfits! And never, ever, ever tell her the outfit she is wearing makes her look fat!)

Scenes from Our Relationship

❖ I am such a casual person that there are countless times I have dressed somewhat inappropriately, if not sloppily. Just the other evening we were due at an event at the local performing arts center, and as we were getting ready to leave, my partner commented, "Do you think those are the right shoes for the slacks you are wearing?" Everyone knows what that implies. Better consider the shined black shoes with the black slacks rather than the scuffed brown shoes worn every day. (You know, the ones with the tiny flecks of paint on them.)

❖ I am the prototypical man with a cowlick. It's like a rooster with a spike of hair on the right side near my part. I welcome my wife letting me know it's sticking up, especially when we are in public settings. She leaves it to me to make the correction, rather than trying to do it herself.

Expand Your Horizons Together

Growth in a relationship does not come from routine, but from finding new adventures or opportunities to share. There are plenty of new things to do together, many of them free, enriching the partnership for both of you.

For most people, a rich full life requires opportunities for excitement. What that means to each couple is infinitely variable. Getting out together and experiencing the world is one of the best ways to maintain a healthy relationship. If you are a dedicated couch potato or a game addict, this may be even truer for you.

Every couple needs new "input" to keep from drowning in the minutiae of daily living. If you want a healthy, interesting life with your partner, then do different things, at least occasionally. Explore the environment you live in, because even a walk around your neighborhood will give you new and varied experiences to discuss. Talk to someone who is different from you—maybe because of a different race or religion, or someone with a tattoo or a ring in their nose. If you are older, make it a point to meet someone young. If you are white, choose a black person. If you speak English, consider someone speaking Spanish or Hebrew or Russian or Arabic. You don't need to be rude or intrusive to do this. It might be easiest to start with someone you meet while doing errands. Even asking an Asian Indian clerk at the post office what they think of the weather will get a response different from that of someone who grew up in your hometown. I started doing this as a kid in a small town in Idaho, and I still do it in the small town where we live. I've done it in all the various places (85 countries and counting) in the world I've traveled.

I should say that I am a dyed-in-the-wool travel addict. My wife says she can tell because I would rather recover from surgery in a foreign country than in my own bed. As a matter of a fact, I once did this while we were traveling in Crete. I may be an extreme case, but I love seeing new places, meeting and interacting with people in other cultures, and experiencing a variety of cuisines. Not everyone can or may want to imitate me, of course, but that doesn't mean there isn't opportunity likely in your immediate geographic area. If you are in New York, Harlem may be unfamiliar ground. If you live in a town, you can explore the countryside. Perhaps there are parks, mountains, lakes, and trails to explore near you. Take a bus to a nearby town and chat with people on the bus. Indeed, get on a local bus and see what that presents. Every town seems to have a farmer's market. People there will live a life perhaps very different from your own, so talk to them about their experience in organic farming. How is cheese made? What's a garlic start? You can ask really simple questions of people you don't know, or even just make comments about the weather, the number of people attending the event, something you are curious about. Surely there are other places both near and far you can explore together.

Or you can create your own new experience. Friends of ours wanted to go to Italy but couldn't afford the trip. So, they got Italian music from the library, ordered movies about Italy, and found four Italian restaurants in a 50-mile radius. They cooked a couple of Italian dinners at home, decorated the dining room like an Italian restaurant, complete with candles, and drank Italian wine. I think they were transported by the experience. However, if you can travel in foreign countries, I especially recommend that. You may make new friends in other parts of the world as we often have. We recently met a delightful couple from Austria—she actually saved my life having been caught in a riptide—with whom we now often communicate through social media.

Exploring new worlds, such as through travel, is often put off until a couple retires. I don't know how many people I've met who have waited for that magic moment, only to discover that one or both cannot physically make the journey. Or they simply don't have, in the final analysis, the needed financial resources. Then they are disappointed that all those great plans and dreams don't happen. Therefore, my advice is to start traveling when you are young, even if that means going only to the next state, county, village, town, or city. It is not just about what you will see and do, but about how you as a couple can grow the relationship through places you experience and people you encounter. You will have more to talk about over dinner with each other and with others, and your conversations are likely to be more interesting and less transactional (e.g., can you pass me the salt? How are the kids doing? Or when will the Mariners game start?). People find you an interesting couple.

Sometimes partners have different reactions to traveling. Our friends include one person who loves to travel, one who hates leaving home, and another who cannot travel for health reasons. One way of still encouraging growth in a partnership where only one spouse really wants to travel is for that spouse to find a traveling companion, perhaps a son or daughter, close friend, in-law or sibling, while the stay-at-home partner can be money and emotional support and enjoying the photos. Virtual travel through exchanged pictures, videos, chats and texts can still make for a kind of shared experience. And these days there are possibilities for shared virtual experiences via the internet, even as you travel. If you are the traveler, once you have gone and returned, you are in a position to share your new friends and new experiences, offering opportunities for learning in personal and collective ways that will add to your development and that of your partner. The best advice I can give you is to start this practice now.

Scenes from Our Relationship

❖ While I could describe numerous travel opportunities my wife and I have taken to expand our horizons together, this one is from everyday living. I am not really much of a bird watcher, although I enjoy observing the annual migration of our state bird, the American Goldfinch. I was happy to let that be my entire birding experience, but my wife kept telling me there was a rockery in our town that was really something. Finally, I relented, and we went down by the city water treatment plant, parked, and walked around to the back of the complex where we found a rockery of blue herons. There must have been 20 nests high in the trees, and occasionally a heron would stick its head out or fly gracefully from or to the nest. So lately we have started to take more notice of the variety of birds in our neighborhood (we live in the midst of a forest, so there is a lot to see). Sitting on the front or back deck takes on a whole new meaning. I just bought a bird field guide, if you can imagine. Sometimes (if not often) I have to get out my characteristic complacency and just go experience things we can then enjoy together.

❖ Like most couples, our entertainment usually takes the form of watching TV or going to an occasional movie. I volunteer at a local vintage movie theatre, so we often see offbeat movies together or with another couple. My wife started getting a little bored with our "usual" entertainment and suggested we expand our horizon to other venues. There is another old theater in town with live performances, so we went recently to hear Ira Glass from "This American Life." Then we went to the performance of a bluegrass group held at a local church venue. There is an improv in town, so that was another option. When you both observe that you have become routine in your collective behavior together, there are probably a great many ways you can explore new horizons.

There's Value In Having a Spiritual Side

Spirituality is about how we see ourselves (individually and together) in the world. It helps us to have a common, shared view, and with it, we can seek harmony with others and especially with our partner.

L et me share with you one of my core beliefs: A spiritual dimension is important for any enduring relationship. I don't care if your belief is based on Sasquatch (though that may be a little far out there) but have some fundamental belief that anchors you in the wonder of the universe we are all part of.

I am not necessarily referring to religion when I say the spiritual side of life, though religion can be a big part of it. Certainly, belief in the divine is important to many, a cornerstone for others, and of no thought to others in a relationship. That's cool. But being spiritual in a broader sense can take many forms. If one form is sharing your common thoughts, beliefs and challenges with one another, you may discover it binds a couple in ways that nothing else will. Virtually anything can be part of your spirituality. Even being part of a medieval jousting group has a certain shared spiritual dimension. Without something that binds us, life is just living. Surely there must be more than that.

Sharing a belief in something fundamental will give meaning to what you do individually and in relationships—with children, family, friends, colleagues, and others in your community. It's a sign that you are not just two people living together, but are an entity, a tangible thing that connects to the world and beyond—the universe if you will—together. You live together with a shared sense of what it means to be and act as a human. And being human is about caring for others, providing for others, acknowledging, and accepting differences—especially your partner's.

 **Scenes from Our Relationship**

❖ My wife and I are Christians. I grew up as a Baptist, although I joined the Quakers for a while, was an elder in the Presbyterian Church, and dabbled a little in evangelical services. My wife is almost a traditional Catholic, but she has a broader faith than most Catholics. What we share and practice together is a basic belief in Jesus Christ. Our spirituality takes the form of regularly attending church and following His example, based on love and helping those in need, especially the poor. Our spiritual side plays out in social justice activities, aiding and caring for others regardless of their sexuality, economic status, race, or any other factor. Therefore, in our life together, we are nice to others, respect their rights, feed them when they need feeding, visit the sick, walk the dying home, provide jackets and socks to the homeless, and generally try to do what Christ would do. The fact that we share a common belief and act accordingly lends great meaning to our personal relationship. Spirituality is the cornerstone of being individuals and a couple. I suspect that a shared belief not grounded in spirituality also works, but I can't really address that from my experience. So whether you are Christian, Muslim, Greek Orthodox, Jewish, Hindu, Buddhist, atheist, or whatever, if you want to have a great relationship with your spouse, look to bolstering your spiritual life with beliefs you share (and act out) with one another, even if you call them by different names, and especially by the actions they prompt you to do together. And that means getting along with others and letting them enrich your life no matter what their spiritual side is.

Words Count

From one's marriage vows to listing what needs to be bought at the grocery store, the words you use make a difference. I advise you to use words carefully, and never as a weapon. That will keep the relationship positive.

Words really do count. If you really don't believe me, just try telling your partner that what they are wearing makes them look dumpy. Or that they are not very smart. Or that they never listen. Or that you're going to the ballgame whether they like it or not. Words have power, so they can hurt, and they can heal. What they do depends on you and your intention in using them. Negative intent hurts any relationship. Positive intent helps build the relationship.

Much of what you say to your partner emanates from another practice already addressed in this book (#5: R-E-S-P-E-C-T). I know that a lot of the words you use can come from your own childhood family dynamics. If your parents argued and were disrespectful to each other and to the children, it's likely you can unconsciously mirror them. Even though you might slip occasionally, your partner will appreciate the effort you make. If you do not want to repeat their mistakes, you can work on being more civil and respectful. A dear friend of mine grew up with his mother saying, "You good for nothing shit. You will never amount to anything." My friend is proud of the fact that he has never once uttered those words to any of his children, grandchildren, or great-grandchildren. I know I've worked to be sure my words are not surly, or offensive, or sharp, even though I grew up in a very healthy family situation and did not have the propensity for mirroring bad parental behavior.

If you discover that you are making personal attacks on another person's character, actions, beliefs, or looks, you need to address this tendency—perhaps with a counselor. Sometimes we finally recognize that we are carrying emotional burdens from our parents, previous marriages, or even from our current partnership. Recognition is a wonderful way to grow personally and do away with those harmful past experiences. But it's pretty impossible to do this alone or even with a loving partner. Remember, your partner is not your therapist. You both can overcome the pain of hot or cruel words in an argument, but it takes work.

Scenes from Our Relationship

❖ One of the more important things I've learned (through two marriages) is that at times I use words that can hurt my partner. Whether I say them jokingly or misuse a word for what I wanted to say, or even something I choose intentionally during an argument, I have come to realize that my hurtful words do hurt. I can actually feel the hurt inside me; so I well know the hurt they must feel. Given this, what I've learned is how to recover from my stupidity. I do this by simply asking, "How did what I just said hurt you?" Note the emphasis here is not on the hurtful word(s) themselves (which I will eventually own up to and deal with), but on the results I can sense (the feeling I caused). Once my partner and I understand the hurt, we can go back to the cause of the hurt and work on how not to repeat the error. I am assuming that you, like me, do not intend to hurt or belittle your partner, or try to "get their goat" or "pull their chain." (If those were your motives, a fast apology is called for.) After the emotions are addressed, the content of the comment can be discussed and resolved. There is no need to continue the fight. I love this approach. It's subtle, but it really works. I recommend you try it for yourself next time this situation presents itself.

PS I give full credit to my partner for teaching me this approach to resolving hurtful words. It's her version of Practice # 45, Do You Want Me to Coach You on That?

❖ I have become very cognizant of how swearing is used so casually in conversations these days. It is not unusual to walk down the street or be sitting in a restaurant and overhear an F-bomb or other words we used to consider foul language. I don't want to seem a prude about this, but it seems that swearing has gotten out of hand and is used more often than needed. Surely there are other words that can as easily connote what one wants to emphasize. In our relationship, we rarely use swear words in everyday conversations and certainly not in arguments. It keeps things civil. Sure, now and then we use a swear word when referring to politics, computers, spills, or our reaction to someone's driving. But never-ever in relationship to one another.

Money, Money, Money

Getting the financial aspects of your relationship in order is critical to happiness. Financial stability allows you to concentrate on other aspects of life; ignoring money and not planning for the future will create or postpone problems that can seriously impact your life.

It has been said, that the three things that cause the most trouble in marriage are sex, religion, and money. I address the first two elsewhere (see #s 33 and 27 respectively). Here, I want to address the issue of the last of the three.

Dealing with the financial approach and everyday practice you'll follow is an absolutely necessary "have to do" discussion that should occur early in a relationship. I advise that you plan this area of your life well. If you are deep into the relationship without really have done so, it's never too late (until retirement). Some people are particularly adept at managing money; others are not. You may both be good at it; in which case you are most fortunate. When one of you is not great with finances, that person must admit it. If both not good at it, then that too. When a partner needs to rely on the other, make sure you still work together. (My wife is very good at financial planning, to my great benefit.) If both of you are inept, professional help—or at least the guidance of a family member or trusted friend—is worth whatever it costs. You can also listen to Dave Ramsey and others on their podcasts, and that may help. The thing is, if you don't get the money under control, not only are you likely to suffer in the present, but you may well end up without sufficient money available to enjoy your golden years (and yes, God willing, they will come one day). It's best to address this issue as soon as possible.

Today, many a man and woman often come into their relationship with debt. There was all that high-cost schooling, delays in becoming an adult, some overspending for personal gratification, and perhaps just bad judgment where money is concerned. We have known people who would not marry until all the debt was gone, which is a great incentive. If one or both of you cannot adequately manage your present budget (let alone the future), then money is a real issue.

I am a no-debt (other than house and car) kind of guy. I pay all my credit card debt on time. But I wasn't much for planning for the future—some regular deposits through various employers' plans, but not much else. This became especially clear when I was in my 50s. I had gotten divorced and was left with few savings, then went into business with my new partner. We had to plan for now and the future (with a much shorter timeline than you might have). Income varies a lot for consultants, freelancers, and others in the gig economy. At the start of our planning, my partner told me a story about a mutual colleague whose situation was similar to ours. As a freelance consultant, this colleague sometimes made plenty of money, then at other times, not so much. She had a good run for several months, so she treated herself to a hugely expensive watch. A few months later, she had virtually no business prospects, no income, and no savings, but she did have a very expensive watch to monitor time in her unhappy situation.

The advice I give can't really address specifics for your given situation, job, opportunity, knowledge, etc., but there are a few basic guidelines that will help in your partnership when it comes to money. First, talk honestly about who is skilled when it comes to money management like spending, paying bills, saving, and being financially literate. Sit down for some businesslike discussions between the two of you, and perhaps with advice that you seek from others (friends or professionals) who have expertise in financial planning and can help you create a clear picture of your income, your expenses, potential emergencies, and so on. In this, you are also assessing one another's financial skills to execute your plan. If you are best at paying bills on time, then that is your job. If they are best at controlling expenses, then that is their job. Don't just assume one or the other will conduct every aspect of financial matters. Don't spend individually on the run as if there were no future. Before you know it, the future is the present. Your money is a mutual responsibility, belonging to both of you, and is a reflection of who you are as a couple. And do not use money as a means of controlling one another. Finances are a partnership based on skills and abilities, recognition of what's real (good or bad), and attempting to let each person have what is important to them. I like to travel, so my wife watches what other expenses we have so that there is money for travel. She might want a newer, spiffier car, but doesn't go there so that we can save every year to get away from bad weather. A good financial relationship requires both of you to participate, so that you have an ongoing sense of what's actually happening and whether you are achieving your mutual goals. This awareness allows you to adjust your behavior as your needs and opportunities change.

Second, you need a budget you're both aware of, written or mutually agreed to, that is real and followed. You are trying to survive financially in a tough world. Along with planned expenses, you will likely be bitten by unexpected emergencies. Before that happens, you will need to have asked yourself what a sudden expense does to the budget. You may want to run a simulation of this possibility by putting funds away and judging the impact when an actual emergency (e.g., the water heater breaks down) requires these funds. Plan and execute for the present, but also plan for emergencies. Nothing reduces stress in a marriage more than being able to say, "We have an account that will cover that!"

Third, work to get debt under control. There is nothing more harmful than too much debt. If you are using more than two credit sources (other than for your house and car[s]), and they have fairly large amounts of debt and/or high interest rates, causing to only pay the interest-only time and time again, then you are unlikely to get ahead—ever! There is plenty written on how to budget, and getting rid of debt can take some sacrifice, but there are plenty of examples of couples who have been successful at eliminating debt. (Ignoring the problem never works.)

Fourth (as if it were as simple as four steps), have a plan for the future and continuously follow it. Frankly, I think this requires the aid of certified experts in the financial planning arena. There is the real difficulty of finding one who is good and won't take advantage of you. Fortunately for us, we found such a person. As basically a nonprofit with great client service, they helped us plan and execute for the future. It worked so well that we are living even larger than we had planned for. You can plan the future yourself, but you might want a professional to lay the groundwork for your eventual retirement. You'll likely need, as I did, to have to get over the fact that you are paying someone your money to help you retain and grow your money but believe me it's worth the investment. We all would like our golden years to become in fact golden, and I believe we all deserve that.

 ## Scenes from Our Relationship

❖ My partner in life and business has always insisted that we put away money as we worked—to have at a minimum of six months' income in the bank in case of a business downturn. She was very insistent about saving for retirement and taking advantage of special retirement accounts the government offers (e.g., a SEP for the self-employed). We are now in our latter years, with a steady income from our retirement savings, so we are doing the things we like to do.

It's a simplification, but my insistence on not having any unsecured debt (for example, paying off credit cards every month and only using two credit cards—one for personal things and one for business expenses), combined with her insistence that we save regularly have allowed us to retire comfortably. I am confident that we will both be able to have what we need to live on until death does us part. We are set financially, we did it without arguing through the many years it took to get here.

❖ My wife sits on the board of a local nonprofit. She discovered while doing so that a fellow board member is an exceptionally good financial coach. She arranged with him a deal in which she gives a donation to the nonprofit if, in return, he gives financial advice to a couple of our relatives, as well as to a friend. It has worked out well for both those served and the nonprofit. Look around for people who seem to have it together when it comes to financial planning and see what they might do for you and others.

The Big Three:
Periods, Pregnancy, and
Menopause

Women experience biological events that men never will. These are fraught with emotional and physical aspects that we men must know about so you can support your partner in dealing with them.

This may not seem like a Practice for men, but your understanding of and ability to support a partner who experiences these will help you both cope that much better. The relationship will definitely be better if you have knowledge on your side.

Men don't have, therefore cannot experience any one of these three biological conditions. We can't possibly ever know what our partner is goes through when she experiences each one. Nor can we as men really do anything about them. We need to understand that we are relegated to expressions of empathy and to supporting any action that provides comfort. You can't fix anything here as if it were a mechanical breakdown on the car. And saying things like "Get over it!" or "What's wrong with you?" won't help a damn bit, but rather exacerbate their negative feelings about you. I will say again and again that it really isn't about you, it's really about them!

What you want to first do is come to some appreciation of what they are going through. There is lots of discomfort physically, as well as mentally, associated with these three biological conditions. Periods often make women moody; pregnancy is a huge discomfort on a nearly continuous basis for nine whole months, and menopause means their emotions will be up and down like the worst of roller coasters. If you wanted to experience something similar, but not exactly, you could attach a 35 lb. hunk of lead to your belly, put a clothes-pin on your penis all day, and have a bloody nose that lasts for seven days. This is, of course, just an approximation of a physical condition that can reoccur every month until late in life, or for nine continuous months when you have shared your sperm or from about age 48 to 51 respectively. Since you will never really experience anyone of the three, your assignment is mostly to sit back, at least understand that their physical and emotional experiences are pretty much out of their control. A shoulder massage, some kind words, some planned diversions, keeping your own emotional reactions at bay, and many other signs and ways of outward sympathy on our part are much needed and appreciated by our partner during these times.

I have gone through all three stages with my two partners. In order of some kind of magnitude I'd rank them from hardest to not really totally easiest to cope with from my vantage point as first, menopause being the hardest, to pregnancy being second (could be ranked one by many), and periods the easiest (an understatement I know!). Of course, your experience will vary depending on your coping mechanism, how you understand what is happening, and your ability to be supportive. For example, if you participate in their pregnancy by attending birthing sessions, being there during the actual delivery itself (if they want you), and then participate in easing the initial shock of being home and participating in the early stages of baby care, you'll gain a better appreciation of what's going on and she will gain a willing partner that she can at least tolerate while feeling lousy. Pregnancy is the only one of the three biological experiences that you can participate in when you really come right down to it. But, the other two—periods and menopause—are part of the birth package. Without her periods, you cannot father a child with her. And menopause is the end of fertility—fertility you may rejoice in as you look at your children, grandchildren, and even great grandchildren. So, get onboard with the pregnancy and participate in the beauty of birth. Relish the idea that menopause will end one day.

When it comes to periods and menopause, each female experience and reacts individually; it's all part of their body/hormone makeup. Some experience relatively easily and less painfully physically and emotionally than others. It may seem as if the person you know has disappeared during select periods (a little play on words) of time. Your first requirement is to realize what is going on (and you may need to ask), then second to not over-react, and finally third to do anything (only in light of what you think she would like; again ask) that might help her deal with the discomfort. Again, the massage, the expressions of empathy with the condition(s) at hand, taking the kids out, letting her sleep in, bringing tea and toast, going to the store and buying the tampons she ran out of, etc. will all help you to maintain being a true partner, while helping her to cope. It's really about your partner and not about you! By the way, buying tampons is not that difficult; you can always use the self-checkout line if that helps your ego. Your problem is really knowing what brand, size, and kind she wants, and you'll likely make a mistake the first time in your purchase! A picture on your iPhone will solve that as well but do plan to erase in case you are showing travel pics to friends, your boss, or family later.

Scenes from Our Relationship

Note: This Scene is best viewed from my partner's perspective of how she counted on me to support her as related to this practice. I remember her taking me on a walk one Spring day and explaining what she would be going through at the onset of menopause. Therefore, I asked her to write this scene.

❖ Guys have it pretty simple—I think of your plumbing and reproductive systems as being a newly-built ranch house. And, a woman's system is like an old beautiful Victorian house, with many colored outside walls, and elaborate layout (with many small rooms) and aging plumbing.

Danny has always been calm in the face of hormone-fueled crankiness. While I often felt that way (guys, you cannot imagine what it feels like to be 5 lbs. heavier today than yesterday, and to find that your favorite slacks don't fit!), he never mentioned hips or tummies. As we married in our 50s, we did not have children together, so pregnancy was not an issue. Sometimes his greatest gift was giving me "space," or a time to be with my women friends. There I could talk about feelings woman to woman.

It's also true that his assumption that all that "women's stuff" was a natural part of life was helpful. He never took my moodiness as a complaint against him. If there was a valid comment from me like, "Can you turn that football game down?" he would address it with no argument.

❖ I (Danny writing) never had the pleasure of being in the delivery room when my two children were born. It was back in the day when such things were not common. These many years later I am disappointed that I wasn't there in the room. One's children are such an important part of our existence as a couple, and to not have shared in some small way in their coming into the world is disappointing. I say this in case you are a guy who could have this experience. Don't pass it up!

A Day (or part of it) for Us

Life, even together, can get to seem like a drag if overloaded with routine. Getting out and doing something together occasionally has a different feel to it and can remind you both of the days when it was just the two of you. Do something to break the routine now and then.

Whether your partnership includes children or not, taking an occasional day (or even a few hours) only with your partner is a must. A date night, a trip to another local city, the Saturday farmers market, or whatever will serve the purpose, as long as it is just the two of you.

It's important in any relationship to realize that always doing the same things can make for a dull partnership. Of course, ordinary things constitute most of our mutual lives. We are making a living, socializing with others, dealing with issues, and meeting life's basic needs. This seems to go on and on and while it can be fulfilling in and of itself, it's often not exciting or a spur to growth. Now and then we need to put all that to the side and concentrate on the two of us and the meaning we have or need to foster in our relationship. Lately, because we are retired and have the time, we have been going to an island in the South Pacific for a few weeks. That is for us, just "living" and being with one-another, taking time out from the day to day. It's not about vacation, which can consist of filling each and every moment of time with activities like parasailing (which I don't do), snorkeling (which I do do), or the numerous things that vacationers feel they must cram into every second. Rather, it's a time we can be with one another, relax, appreciate the beauty and weather, take long walks along the beach, sit in lawn chairs in the water near shore, soak in some culture, and make new, if temporary, friends (hopefully from other countries). We even fold in a little writing and art, but we don't let those activities consume our being together. They are just minor diversions of our attention to one another, and not the kind of thing we would do if we were home.

Thus, the "date night/togetherness," or whatever you would choose to call it, becomes a special event that centers on the two of you together. It can be a park in your neighborhood or an island in some dreamy place. Whatever and wherever, try it! Don't get so caught up in everyday life so exclusively that you fail to honor your mutual presence in the world.

 **Scenes from Our Relationship**

❖ We own an old Miata, so recently, on a warm Sunday, we put the top down and drove along the Washington coast. We stopped at a local seafood farm to enhance the experience over some fresh clams and a beer. It gave us an opportunity to do something we have since come to love doing now and then.

❖ We go through periods of doing various kind of activity. Another recent day we started exploring the many local micro-breweries that dot our community. Other days we try a new restaurant for some appetizers, then perhaps have dinner or go to a movie at the independent film center where I volunteer. We even found an old fashion burger joint where they take orders at window side. On these occasions we generally talk about our separate and combined lives, the past week, and our future plans in a new setting, which can provide fresh inspiration. Mix in a little or lot of how we appreciate one another and our life together, and it can be a perfect day unlike any other.

Be Kind

Just being kind to one another seems as if it should be a given, but it turns out that it can take a conscious effort to be kind. What you do or don't do, as well as what you say or don't say (practice #28, Words Count) have a great deal to do with how your partner sees you. Learn to be kind in all you do.

s I wrote this part of this book, I was on a cruise sitting with my wife and a couple from Indiana whom we just met over breakfast. We found out that he had a PhD in our own field, and we were even able to share thoughts about a mutual professional friend. We were talking in general about many topics (including my writing this book) when I turned to his wife and asked, "What makes your husband a good husband?" She immediately replied, without hesitation, "He's a very kind man!" As I had talked to him and observed his general demeanor and tone of conversation with his wife, I had seen that his actions and his words were indeed kind. She reflected his kindness back to him, which is a foundational practice in any healthy relationship (with partner or others), and it was easy to tell how happy they were with one another.

Kindness is kind of an old-fashion virtue in this day and age. Given social media, one can easily express all the unkindness that they may have pent up, but that doesn't make it right—especially when in a person-to-person relationship. Kindness is really the opposite of cruelty, but it can also be seen as one of the opposites of rudeness (another is politeness), but kindness is deeper than politeness. Rudeness and cruelty do not have any place in a healthy relationship.

Fundamentally, kindness is a behavior that our parents (if they were inclined themselves) admonished us to learn growing up, but, if not present for whatever reasons, it can be developed. In my family, kindness was always promoted as a virtue. In my wife's, by her own admission, it wasn't always so. Unfortunately, kindness is not born in us. It is not an "attribute," which are those elements that we are born with. The importance of this distinction—between innate (born with) versus that which can be learned—is the difference between nature and nurture. Kindness can be nurtured; thus, there is hope for those in a relationship where kindness seems to be lacking. We can all get better at kindness.

The level and degree of kindness in my marriage is very high. This is because we both have a great deal of love and respect (practice # 5, Respect) for one another, so our kindness stems from a base of mutual respect and admiration (practice # 42, I Think She is Wonderful). We show this by making sure that what we do and how we use words, even when we differ, are not hurtful to one another. Thus, I know she is kind to me, and I am kind to her.

Kindness is particularly important during times of disagreement. Thus, even though I might differ with her approach to something we are going to do or how we view something (e.g., politics), I avoid unkind words to bolster my point of view. I also watch my tone of voice. I know that raising my voice to make my point will just exacerbate the interaction and limit any solution—in short, yelling never helps. I do get into trouble sometimes around kindness when I am joking about something, and she doesn't realize what I'm doing. This is something I am working on to make better—yes, I am still learning kindness.

We can all be aware of times when we need to learn to use words that are kinder. As an extreme case, the other day I had just passed the screening point at TSA in our local airport when I observed an elderly husband verbally berating his wife, ordering her to hurry up as they exited the screening area. She was nearly in tears and told him, "Just tell me what to do, and I'll do it." He needed to be told that his words were unkind. She needed to be more insistent that he does not use such words.

Here are a couple of useful guidelines in becoming kinder:

Don't *say* unkind things, such as:

- That's a stupid notion!
- What's wrong with you?
- Don't you know anything?
- Where did you get that idea?
- Were you born in a barn?
- Can't you see it—it's right in front of your face!
- They are not very quick when it comes to things.

Don't *do* unkind things, such as:

- Ignoring your partner's input
- Acting as if they are not very smart
- Insulting what your partner cooks or does
- Withholding money
- Disparaging your partner in front of friends or relatives
- Comparing your partner unfavorably to others

 **Scenes from Our Relationship**

❖ As I was getting out of bed one Sunday morning into a dreary day of rain and clouds, I thought to myself that it would be kind of me to go retrieve the two morning papers we subscribe to, get my wife a cup of her favorite tea, and present all of this to her in bed. I did, and she was delighted. It was a simple act of kindness for someone I like to treat special. I'd like to think that my level of kindness, however, is not so much about my actions, but rather is shown in my general daily demeanor toward my partner. If she wants me to do something for her, I try my best to accommodate it as soon as I can. I don't say, "Don't bother me, I am too busy to help you!" Want something fixed? I am there. Want me to comment or help frame a piece of art she has composed? I'll do it. As I said elsewhere, I am her ATM: Any Time Man. That is an attitude; it's not that I am somehow her slave or better than her. I believe in helping others, and especially my partner. Kindness stems from attitude and action. It's a behavior you can learn, practice, and get rewarded for.

❖ I like to write a lot. I have penned several books, numerous professional articles, and given lots of presentations here and abroad. One of my partner's sheer acts of kindness is her willingness to edit everything I write. One might think this is charity or kindness on her part since I write very long sentences (think 50 words or so) that need shortening to be readable. Indeed, a boss once said to me, "You should have been born as a conjoined twin, so your brother could have been your editor!" Instead, I married a woman who skillfully and cheerfully (most of the time) edits my work. It is a challenge for her, I realize, since she has to get into my head to determine what I am trying to say, and then offer a way to do that more elegantly or accurately. I know I am competing with her artwork. Her kindness is appreciated. And, I might add, you are benefiting from it as you read this book. You should thank her for her kindness! I know I do.

Sex and Sensuality
In Relationship

Sex in a relationship is easy, but sensuality is equally, if not more, important and can be more difficult to know how to actualize. What is the difference? What can you do to be mutually satisfied if aging or other conditions make sex impossible?

Sex is, for many if not most, the most important aspect of their relationship. There is no question that it is enjoyable, filled with heightened emotion, and emblematic of being a couple. Having said that, frankly sex rates about third on the scale of what makes for a really loving, compatible, and complete union with your partner. Perhaps one can only really understand this when either you lose your sexual prowess or find it less compelling due to age or physical limitations. Seen in the light of not being able to have sex as one used to, you might ask "What's left? And how do I make it as good as what we had when sex was an important part of the relationship?" The answer to this question likely reveals what's really vital to you and your partner: Is it sex or other things?

Life can be lonely if you don't have relationships with others. That is why friends and family are important to us social beings. This is especially true when it comes to a partner—the one you are or can be closest with. It's therefore incumbent upon us to make that partnership as meaningful and full as possible. We do this by the way we treat one another far more than by the sex we have—although sex obviously helps. Believe it or not, one can do without sex, but doing without relationship is almost unthinkable. Therefore, you need to make your relationship a priority. To that end, sensuality can be an important ingredient whether or not sex is a part of it.

Sensuality means feelings that come when we touch others physically and emotionally. You might think of it as virtually anything that leads up to but doesn't include the sex act (obviously that it quite sensual itself). The division here is made only to indicate that everything leading up to sex is still possible even when sex is not and can play an important part in the relationship. Freely exploring sensuality with your partner is key to having a secure and satisfying overall relationship. It can be as easy as hugs, as discovering what makes your partner feel physically treasured, as exploring touch. What are the best times to do any of these? What kind of exploration do you and your partner want? (Using objects for such will not be discussed here, but for some it plays a role.)

Sex and/or sensuality are, when you distill them down objectively (if we ever do), a basic form of communication in a relationship. They are a way of saying "I am in contact with you, my partner" without using words (though you can certainly talk if you want to during acts of being sensual). Those who think sex is purely physical are missing its most meaningful power by relegating it to a solely physical act without additional benefits in enriching the relationship itself. You and your partner are really missing something that is very important. Give it thought next time and commit to convincing your partner that you really like touching them for reasons other than foreplay. They will appreciate that more than you know!

 **Scenes from Our Relationship**

❖ Several years ago, I learned that I had cancer of the prostate. When that happens, the more than 80% of men who live long enough to develop it have only a few choices to treat the cancer. These include surgery, chemo, watchful waiting/active surveillance, radiation, ultrasound, hormone therapy, freezing, and vaccine therapy. Each choice has pitfalls, so men choose what they individually believe is best for them given their age, progression of the cancer, and so forth. Given how my cancer was positioned, I opted for surgery to remove the prostate; I have never regretted that decision. I don't have or will ever again have that dreaded form of cancer. But it did affect my sexual performance. Recognizing this, I have committed to sensuality as a substitute. My partner has been accepting of that, and we enjoy our intimate times together. Enough said.

❖ Every morning, I find my wife sitting at the kitchen table. She generally gets up earlier than I and so it is not unusual to find her there doing some journaling, reading the paper, studying art techniques, or catching up on correspondence with people around the world. While we have usually already talked in bed to start the morning (see practice #4, Starting The Day Together), as I pass her I touch her, usually on her shoulder; she responds with appreciation. Other times, I lean over and give her a kiss on the back of her neck. These are all signs of sensuality amid everyday living.

Learn To Read
The Nonverbals

What's in a frown? In a smile? What does it mean when your partner looks away? Their body language is far more important than you may realize. If you can learn to read the cues they give you without words, you may avoid misunderstandings or realize new adventures.

We travel a lot, and if there is one thing I truly enjoy to pass the time in airports, cafes, waiting for an Uber driver, at museums, or just killing time somewhere on a park bench, it is people-watching. I am fascinated by how someone interacts with a partner, children, and others. I try to guess what they are thinking and what seems to frustrate them by being aware of what they are doing. I often ask my wife, "What do you think that couple is thinking?" Sometimes the answer seems written clearly on their faces and shown by their communication with others—especially a spouse. While much of what I conclude is indicated by what they say, a lot can also be read by the outward visual, tactile, and kinesthetic channels of communication everyone employs.

By definition, nonverbal cues include anything we do that communicates to others without involving or using words or speech. Gestures mean things. A raised eyebrow, a grin, a blush, and a grunt are subtle, while throwing up arms, turning away, and stomping out of the room are more obvious. All these gestures mean something. They can be either understood or confusing. You and your partner often use these ways of communicating, even when you choose to ignore them. When you use them, you are conveying to others positive or negative emotions. Being able to "read" or discern the meaning behind your partner's nonverbal cues is as important for your communication as the words you say. Misreading those cues can lead to real trouble. (Just ask a husband who has misread his partner concerning an anniversary dinner versus, say, going to a ballgame on the anniversary date).

In a healthy relationship, you have made an effort to read, understand, and act on the implied means of your partner's nonverbal communication. We can't just rely upon verbal communication, and if we are, a whole dimension of understanding is missing. This is true if for no other reason than that sometimes people tell us what we want to hear them say but contradict the words by their body language. For example, you ask your partner to go to a ballgame, and they say, "Yes!" while shrugging their shoulders. Does this mean they want to go or has just given up on saying, "No, I'd rather do something else." We learn a great deal when we compare actions with what is said, and all we have to do is ask ourselves to pay attention to what our partner's demeanor says that the words may not convey.

All of us need to look for nonverbal cues and learn to react to them. Doing so will help our relationships in numerous ways. Failing to read them accurately can be taken to mean you don't care enough about your partner's feelings.

Before I give you some personal examples, the general classes of nonverbal cues that you should pay attention to include:

- Personal space
- Posture
- Mode of dress
- Touch
- Eye gaze

 **Scenes from Our Relationship**

❖ At least twice a year, we go with our best friends (see practice # 35, Have a Few Really Good Friends) to a Seattle Mariners baseball game. Our friend's wife has a medical condition that can make her very tired, so we all understand that when she is tired, we leave the game early—whether the Mariners are ahead or not. She usually does not want to spoil our fun, so she won't complain. In order to take care of her, we pay attention to her body language—i.e., when she looks kind of tired, or the conversation has waned a little, or she glances at her watch, we can say that we'd like to beat the traffic conditions that always occur at game's end.

For my part, I am also looking at my partner's nonverbal cues. She isn't a rabid fan of baseball, and so when I think she looks like she has had enough, I am comfortable asking her if she is ready to leave. Besides, we can always stop on the way home for something like dinner.

❖ My partner reads my nonverbals as if she were casually reading a technical manual on nuclear physics. She seems to know what I mean, even when I haven't said it. For example, she will ask me a question about going somewhere with her and I'll typically say, "Yes," but she knows not to let that answer be so easy. She sees an expression on my face, the slowness with which I answer, or the even the tone of my answer and realizes that I am agreeing in order to not disagree. So she follows up with a question to find my real answer, e.g., "Are you busy with other things?" "How does doing that work into your plans for the day?" She has my number and is not shy about dialing-up some questioning and exploring my real feelings and meaning. It is not that I am trying to hide my emotions, it's just that I often "go along to get along." I like harmony in my life, so I try to be agreeable. But my outward actions can tell a different story. That is where facial expressions, tone of voice, and even posture tell the real story. I do try to read her nonverbals as well, but she is definitely better at doing so.

Have a Few
Really Good Couple Friends

A couple should not live in a vacuum. Couples can increase their activities by sharing them with other, like-minded couples who are good friends. All your lives can be enriched by celebrating the big occasions and experiencing the little ones in each other's company.

A s much as we may love our partner, we need other people to enrich us both individually and as a couple. It is best to choose and nurture these special friends with great care as they become a kind of extended family, and it's best when they can be a family that you can truly count on to be faithful, nurturing, discreet, and fun.

I encourage you to find and nurture friends (married or single) in general, but to encourage really close relationships with a few other couples. This can raise a few questions. Will those you are closest to be your friends or your partner's friends? Or can you find couples who are both of yours? I suggest that you try to build mutual friendships that can reward both of you, because if they are only your or your partner's friends, they come with their own baggage and may think only about one of you, rather than seeing you as a single entity. I'm not saying this kind of relationship can't work with someone who knew one of you, perhaps before you and your partner were together, but it's just usually better if they now like both of you.

Naturally, guys gravitate to guys, and women gravitate to women. I suspect it's generally harder for men to meet couples who may be good candidates for this close relationship. That's because men tend to gravitate to others they drink with, go to sports games, know from work, or perhaps are life-long friends. Women often prefer those who share their own present activities or workplaces. These don't automatically qualify as the kinds of friends that will work for you as a couple. Also, when men have female friends or women have male friends there can be a suspicion that there could be threats to a partnership. And though any human who clearly knows boundaries and how to maintain them could have a friend of the other sex, sometimes their partner is uncomfortable. But for purposes of this practice, let's stick to couples befriending other couples. With that in mind, here is some advice about the kinds of friends to look for and foster the relationship.

The special couples you choose should be the kind of friends who really enhance your own relationship. They may do this through their love of you, but they can also share the same tastes, the same ethics, the same stage of life or spirituality. Further, such friendships allow you to learn from and be entertained by each other. You get to see them up close, as they handle such life issues as conflict. For example, my wife and I have one particular set of good friends, and one of them, Clairene, has a cute way of calling her husband, "Hey, Dude," when he annoys her. He gets it and stops whatever he was doing. We learned from them (even though I can't imagine my wife calling me "Dude" in any circumstance) that signals can be nonthreatening and still work, that annoyance can be expressed without leading to anger. Learning from one another can create a mutual admiration society that makes all four of you better. Most couples can generally accommodate upwards of two to four sets of such mutual friends in their extended family. After that number it becomes a crowd.

Whenever you are developing a relationship with a new couple, a "vetting" process needs to take place before you and they have the prized status of mutual friends. You need to plan and execute events wherein you and your partner "try out" another couple's friendship. And you both have to come to a conclusion that these friends will work for both of you. If not, and they can be an acquaintance of one of you; that's okay. There are lots of potential mutual friends out there, and you both have to continue to look and try them on for size. For the reasons I've already mentioned, finding mutual friends usually works best from a clean slate. They will be new sets of people you encounter together in different settings: in church, at a social event, on a cruise, from among your neighbors, at entertainment venues, or in other places where couples gather. They might be a couple you happen to share a table with at a local brewery, and you click and want to get together again. Once you have met new people, you will be able to move into a closer relationship with them. You and they can become a new and enduring family with whom you and your partner can have a special, enriching friendship.

 ## Scenes from Our Relationship

❖ We have two particular sets of couple friends whom we simply adore and can't wait to do things with. One set lives not far from us. We often get together to share appetizers and drinks at our homes, go out to dinner, attend a baseball game, and have traveled together to Iceland and Spain. Bob is a card, funny and outgoing. He seeks out interesting people, places, and experiences. He's always trying new things, talking to someone about their tattoos or nose rings, and he organizes our men's lunch group (called ROMEO: Retired Old Men Eating Out). His partner, Clairene, whom I mentioned above, is a charmer. I had got to originally know her and eight other women in a spiritual discussion group centered on social justice. She and I formed our own bond, which my wife knew about and supported. When we first got together as two couples, we discovered we were fortunate to share lively conversation, mutual interests, and profound respect for one another—we even liked their really squirrelly dog, Bella.

❖ Our second set of really close friends lives on an island. Dora is a local; she knows the history of her island people and shares fascinating stories about her family and culture. She is also an artist who sews beautiful garments and traditional pillow covers for sale in the local market. As artists, her and my wife share many aspects of their lives between them. Her husband, Glynne, is our funny man. With a dry sense of humor like my own, he exudes fun and drops pearls of historical facts from his deep reservoir of knowledge. Originally from Wales, he met and married his island beauty nearly 60 years ago. We share "taco night" every week we are on the island, and we reignite the enjoyment we have about being together. We often talk these days on social media.

There is much to be noted in these two brief descriptions. The first is that we all enjoy being with each other. We like each other as human beings, share mutual values, and even our political views match. Second, we laugh a great deal. We tell interesting stories, share experiences, sometimes travel together, and poke fun at ourselves and the funny circumstances we have faced. And third, we are confident that we can share personal thoughts that will go no further than the front door.

Jointly Do Something For Humanity

Enhancing your life by doing something worthwhile for humanity gives a couple a sense of purpose beyond themselves. It's a way for you to work together for the greater good of society and your partnership.

y mother was the consummate volunteer in her community. If she wasn't helping the Boy Scouts, then it was perhaps a community organization or church event that used her excellent planning and execution skills. For example, she had six hospital-type beds that she loaned out to anyone in need for convalescence or final days of dying. She gave bags of groceries to those she saw in need of some support. It's no wonder I got the idea of being of service to others from her many examples.

I will always remember the time my mother had me go with her to the local hospital for one of her volunteer efforts. It was during the polio epidemic in the US, and I saw people in full-body ventilators struggling to breathe. She would provide comfort by reading to them or just talking. While there, I learned that the children's waiting room was in need of a new record player, and so I organized my Boy Scout patrol group to collect hundreds of wire hangers to redeem for one cent each at a local dry cleaner. We were able to purchase a new player and lots of children's story albums. I saw firsthand how good that made me and others feel.

There are plenty of volunteer activities that you can, of course, do by yourself. However, I'd like to emphasize community activity for the two of you together. The purpose is clear: You demonstrate both to yourself and to one another that you care for others. You use some of the skills you each have, but together. You are reaching beyond self to serving others for whatever motivates both of you; you may long to reduce the suffering of others, or to participate in your community and meet other likeminded people (see practice # 35, Have a Few Good Couple Friends). You are contributing to society, rather than merely taking or existing in it.

 **Scenes from Our Relationship**

❖ Our community is rich in ways of helping others. One of the more outstanding activities is an annual program of free services provided to our homeless community. This includes dental, legal, vision, hearing, housing, employment, and many other services. Some 500 people make use of these free services annually. My wife and I are in charge of a 30-volunteer contingent who serve a full breakfast and lunch, plus snacks. She uses her excellent facilitation skills to run the orientation sessions and manage volunteer needs as they arise. I organize prepacked lunch distribution to the numerous volunteers serving our clientele. We come away with a wonderful feeling of having served people who express their deep gratitude for what is being done for them. As a couple, we did it together.

❖ There is another community effort for the homeless that involves serving a hot lunch once a month through our local church. It feeds about 300+ individuals a full lunch with desert and offers takeout. I love washing dishes, so that is my assignment. I also currently serve on the board of directors. My wife prefers working the line that serves the hot cafeteria-style meal. There she can enjoy interacting with those coming through the line. We gain a deeper understanding of the needs of others, and a joint activity that gives our own relationship a boost in gratitude for all we have. We have met so many interesting people through this joint effort.

Patience: She Is Only Going to Be Ready When She Is Ready

You're waiting at the door, car keys in your hand. You might as well relax—she will be ready when she's ready. There are reasons for her timing being different from yours, in this case and in others; it helps if you recognize what they are rather than being antsy and irritating.

*P*atience is one key to a successful partnership. It requires discipline because it may not seem natural, and it is so easy to disregard. One common enemy of patience is the difference between men and women when it comes to the preparation to go out. Women usually have many more elements to take care of while dressing and preening. We men generally have fewer items of clothing, fewer body parts to shape up, and fewer decisions among different styles. Tie or not? Blue shirt or white? That's about it, so no wonder we can be ready in minutes while our partners always seem to need a minimum of 30 minutes. This is an opportunity to learn the kind of patience that will be useful in other circumstances. Just relax, men. It isn't likely to go any quicker just because you want it to. Go out and pick a few weeds or even wash the car. She will be ready when she is ready! And, that's really okay. Besides, what were you going to do if you got there any earlier? (If you're going to an event with a concrete start time, for example, the theatre, set an earlier time to begin getting ready.)

Scenes from Our Relationship

❖ We were going out to dinner with good friends with whom we traveled to Europe. We were both getting ready. She had already had fingernails and toes done at the local salon, so we started getting dressed at the same time. Within 10 minutes, I had put on a clean dress shirt, my slacks and shoes and put the car keys in my pocket. She was still trying on different outfits to decide what would work best for the occasion. Typically, she asked me to evaluate each, and I carefully did so. After another 15 to 20 minutes she decided on an outfit and turned to the choice of shoes. She tried on and rejected four or five options, then chose the most appropriate for the weather, the venue, the outfit, and the degree of comfort. Next, she had to fix her hair, do a last-minute rethink on the shoes, and a full-length mirror check on the whole package. I thought we are ready to go out the door, but then she made a stop for a final lipstick application, had to choose a coat, find her reading glasses, select appropriate and matching purse, and find the earrings that had been missing that she wanted to wear.

I learned early on in our relationship that this was her habit, and I was not going to change it. So, when we are getting ready to go out, I do not to stand by the garage door as if I am anxiously awaiting her to be ready. I try not to pace around or ask questions about how long she is going to be. I am Mr. Patience in the background, and it's a role that took several years to develop. Even now, I sometimes slip and look at my watch (see practice # 34, Learn to Read Nonverbals) and hope she didn't notice. There's also a look I seem to have on my face often that I've not learned to hide very well. I realized it's probably better for me to be in the next room, if not out in the garden picking weeds. It's a ritual, one way or another, that we play out many times a year, and we know our roles and rules of engagement. It's a part of our relationship that works because I've learned the value of my patience.

❖ We live a few miles out of town and usually drive in together even if we have separate things to do. She often meets a friend for a walk while I have errands to run. One of things I've learned is that even though she has set up a schedule and I think we will be leaving at a given time, I can't really take that schedule as set in cement. That's because things in her life have a way of changing much more readily than my own. The friend she was going to meet at 2:30 can't get there until at least 3:00, she has an unexpected extra stop to make, and/or she forgot about a conflicting appointment. That is just the way her life works. I've learned to get used to it and not fuss, but instead be flexible. In the grand scheme of things, being flexible isn't really all that difficult. I can always find something else to occupy my time while in town.

Relatives, Neighbors and Friends

The other people who have an effect on a partnership usually fall into three categories: relatives, who can be a pain; neighbors, who can be irritating; and friends, who are most often a source of great joy. You don't need to respond to them all the same way.

There are three groups of people in our lives (by marriage, by proximity, or by choice) who can show us the degree of tolerance we have as a couple. Relatives are often the most difficult to tolerate, followed by neighbors, and finally friends whom we have carefully chosen, and like to do things with. If we get a combination of good neighbors and friends, we are just lucky. We are, by the way, one such lucky couple with good friends and neighbors.

I, for one, think relatives are overrated. There are several I like and some I tolerate, which may well be normal for everyone. Relatives seem to feel completely free to express their opinions regardless of our feelings. In other words, relatives are usually not as polite as friends are. Simply by sharing a bloodline, or because of past history they believe they can make us pay for what they perceive are mistakes made decades ago. Too many people also believe that their parenting obligations extend into their children's 40s and 50s, which can cause really uncomfortable situations. Too much childhood history combined with some negative emotions can cause discord when families get together. My wife always says, "That's why 'Family' always begins with a big F!" (Let's assume that means Freaky). Relatives can have an adverse impact on a couple's own relationship, which hardly seems fair and, in truth, isn't. This can lead to such outbursts as: "Your mother doesn't like me!" "Your brother is such a jerk!" "Do they really have to come for Thanksgiving?"

It is okay to disassociate from or severely limit contact with relatives you or your partner don't like. A partner whose brother, sister, or child is the problem should support the other partner's feelings when those feelings are well founded. Recognize that your partnership first and foremost is about the two of you, a new level of commitment taking precedence over a previous familial relationship. ("Sister, if you can't stand my husband, we will have to minimize our contact." "Dad, he is my husband and you'll have to find ways to get along or we won't come over!") Relatives can be treated just like regular people whom you accept, and reject based on your criteria; they are not individuals who are somehow acceptable because they share your genes. And, of course, you are not required to like your own relatives, so you are certainly not required to like each other's. We *are* commanded to love them, so we need to consider using respect and kindness and meet real obligations to them, like attending funerals or marriages.

Neighbors are different. Neighbors are usually not our relatives, and so we might end up liking them a little more. Unless we choose to relocate, we are stuck with the people next door. Here you may need to overlook some things that your neighbors do that you don't like. Could be their dog, the camper constantly in the driveway, or whatever. It's important to, "know when to hold 'em, know when to fold 'em, and know when to walk away" as Kenny Rogers tells us in one of my favorite country and western songs. If you are fortunate, you and your neighbors can find ways to be pleasant, support one another, and look after one another.

Friends are the best part of relationship with others. We choose these people for their similarity (or differences) to us, shared values and interests, the fun we have together, social and emotional support we give each other, and a host of other characteristics that draw us to them and them to us. A lot of times it's wives to wives, husbands to husbands, or mutual interests in golf, hunting, tennis, gardening, chess, or whatever. We travel to local restaurants and other countries with our friends. One friend's wife helped my wife develop a tolerance for baseball and then an appreciation for and enjoyment of pro ball games in general. We laugh a great deal, celebrate life, and share sadness over illness or death. By definition, that's what friends are!

Here are some helpful rules:

- You don't have to like all the same people.
- Neither do you have to participate with them. But it is best not to just reject them because you don't like them. You need to make an effort.
- Your partner values certain friends, and you need to respect that.

Scenes from Our Relationship

❖ When we started out, we each had a widowed mother and two adult children, and I had two grandchildren. We lost our mothers over the next two decades, lost one child to cancer, kids gained new partners, and we gained seven grandchildren and one great grandchild. We also had a total of seven siblings between us and had occasion to visit them all for varying periods of time. Naturally, we liked some more than others, but we decided to treat our relatives the same way we would treat anyone not related to us, and that has worked out well.

❖ Our neighborhood is filled with people whom my partner and I like, but we associate more with some than others. We all share keys to our homes, so that we can look after one another's things, pick up their mail when away, get a needed onion for cooking, and water plants as needed. We occasionally visit out front, then go on with our individual lives. Some bring us fresh crab when they are out fishing, and we occasionally give them vegetables from our garden.

One even comes over and clears out the poop her cat leaves in our front yard. We don't have to associate with one another, but we do a bit. We have had what we refer to as "Half-a-Block Parties" to catch up with one another after a long winter. So, we are lucky to have such good neighbors.

❖ I have a couple of close friends, but my wife has many. So, I borrow certain of her friends all the time, generally over some mutual activity. I have chosen to accept her friends because she is quite good at fostering and developing rewarding friendships. I trust her word on what they are like and where I disagree, she knows it, accepts, and minimizes such contact. She is respectful of my feelings when it comes to mutual friends, and I am respectful of her feelings. We have some really close friends that we both love and cherish (see practice # 35, Have a Few Really Good Couple Friends).

Putting Your Partner In the Conversation

You and your partner need to communicate within and outside your union. Knowing how to get into conversions with others builds your relationship and exhibits you as equals.

I am, by nature, a fairly quiet person. I am prone to watch and listen more than talk. The downside is that people don't generally get to know me as well as they could if I simply talked more. Recognizing this, I try on occasion to assert myself by either "talking up" or asking questions that help me participate more in an ongoing conversation. That works pretty well, and I can generally be okay with it. However, even I get tired of only listening to people. And once I've repeatedly heard my wife's stories—say, about our trip to Kuwait, or certain other things—I feel the need to participate more in the conversation.

You too may be the quiet one in your relationship—or perhaps it's your partner. They say opposites attract; so I've observed many couples—straight and gay—where one is talkative (the extrovert) and the other is quiet (the introvert). I realize that a person cannot change the essence of who they are. But free speech and the general rules of good relationships demand a change of practice, regardless if you the talkative or the silent one. Otherwise, you are disregarding—or watching your partner disregard—something important: namely, sharing each other's thoughts and feelings about a wide range of things. Nothing quite like being around another person who doesn't have much to say! Or, for that matter, is too talkative. Thus, along the way, I observed my tendency toward silence and learned how to be more engaged in social interactions, let alone in personal conversations with my wife. I did not want to be seen as a stone to my wife's bubbling brook (no criticism intended as I love what she has to say). I have learned that there are three good ways to get you and your partner into a conversation. I will detail them below.

But before I do, I want to indicate how involving your partner in conversation could make a difference in your relationship. First, it always helps to be seen in a good light by others. "Your husband is charming," as opposed to, "How can you stand living with such a quiet guy?" Second, being more talkative takes some pressure off your partner. Why should they always be the socializer? Ask yourself, "What do I bring to the table?" And finally, when you both participate it just feels more equal—to them, to you, and to others.

Scenes from Our Relationship

❖ Speak Up

My first lesson for getting into a conversation in any social situation was to learn to speak up. I know that sounds rather obvious now, but I had to force myself to get out of my comfort zone of just listening. When I find that I am standing or sitting there listening to an interesting conversation, I tell myself to say something. I start to think of how the conversation relates to my own experiences and say something like, "You know, I experienced the same thing and here is what I felt and did about that." That most often gets a reaction, and I am asked something by others in the group. Then we are off and running.

❖ Ask a Question

The other evening, we were at a neighborhood get-together and as is often the case, the guys were talking to the guys and the women to the women. I enjoy being around women a lot, so I stood on the perimeter of that group and listened for a while. They were talking about an issue in our homeowners' association and thus the conversation was lively. I realized that I wasn't saying anything, and so to get out my funk I asked a question: "Why do people in our association so resist the rules (covenants) that we all agreed to abide by when we bought our homes here?" Well, that got the group going, and I had opinions about the topic and joined in. Often as not, if you are quiet like me, you just have to force yourself to join in. If you don't have something relevant to say (approach suggested above), the next easiest way to engage is to ask a question.

❖ Set a Context for Your Partner to Speak

The third approach is directed at getting your partner into the conversation. You can say something that will encourage your partner to speak if they are not doing so. Now obviously this has a potential downside to it—your partner may not feel like talking. I can identify with that because I often feel the same, but I am trying to get over those feelings. I know that my partner has good intentions. She is not trying to embarrass me or make me look bad. She wants me to engage because she knows I know things. So, the key here is to make sure that what you are asking your partner to talk about is something that they have knowledge of and experience with.

My wife's approach to being inclusionary is a direct one: "Danny has some experience in that topic. He was in the Peace Corps in Ethiopia and has intimate knowledge of other cultures." Or, "He grew up in a junkyard environment as a boy, so he knows something about fixing things." Such introductions during an ongoing conversation she is primarily engaged in—and she is a person who can carry on any conversation—are aimed at getting me involved and helping the group at hand understand that I can engage knowledgeably. Her approach also shows that we are partners who value each other's opinion. I have taught myself to try to follow her lead and include her on other occasions in my conversations with others. It's a mutual respect of one another that fosters our shared relationship with others. Other people recognize that we are a couple who value each other's opinion and experiences. So, if you are the dominant one during conversations, make a concerted effort to invite your "silent" partner in.

Commitment Is Stronger Than Non-Commitment

Just like having a deed to your home or a lease on your apartment tells you that you have rights and responsibilities, your marriage ceremony or mutual promises commit you to certain obligations.

e know that legal, formal marriage is not the big thing it once was, but commitment can be present without a legal contract. You can still make, and honor promises to each other, as well as make children and establish a home together. Those vows or covenants are bigger and deeper than contracts. Sure, you can divorce, and many do (take me, for example), but when you formally commit to the other person, it obligates you to try to make the relationship really work. Or, at least a concerted effort to make it work and not just take advantage of a relationship you don't take that seriously.

Commitment can be pretty simple in terms of daily practice. You consider the desired outcome (a happy life) and perform the daily actions that can help lead to it. I've discussed the daily actions (aka Practices) throughout this book. They can be subsumed under practice #32, Be Kind, whenever possible. Kindness can mean politely opening the door for her or carrying heavy bags. But it can also mean lighting a fire in the fireplace when it is cold outside or picking up something they need on your way home. It can also mean being sure they have money on hand to buy things and gas in the car, keeping them from having to nag at you to do something that needs doing. If it is important to your partner, give it priority in your own life and making time for it is a wonderful realization of kindness. Many of these may be little things, but each tells your partner they are important to you and confirms to that you will be around if things get tough.

Commitment shows in the way you comport yourself. It telegraphs to others how you feel about each other. For example, it's fine, as a man, if you look at a pretty woman walking down the street. But it's better not to stare, as that may make your partner feel uncomfortable, even a little jealous. My partner is the only truly pretty woman to me, and I want her to be confident that I feel that way. And, that takes action on my part. To me, that's just one of the many things that commitment means.

Scenes from Our Relationship

❖ By way of an analogy about commitment, I'd like to describe something that happened in the early days of our marriage.

For one year, we rented a very nice four-story contemporary condo in a 12-unit complex in Santa Monica, California. Each condo was laid out exactly the same and reflected the style we wanted to live and ultimately also work in. Our condo was Unit D in the building at 1330. It was very comfortable, but since we rented, we could not change it to make it truly our own, so it felt very temporary to both of us. We could not paint the walls the colors we wanted, put down carpeting, nail picture hooks where we wanted, take out a wall to make a larger room, or the countless other actions we imagined to shape the space around us to our liking. Living there was fine, but we both knew the rental contract for this condo meant it wasn't really ours, and we could leave it any time we wanted.

As it happened, the opportunity rose to buy another of the 12 condos, because we happened to own a house in a town 80 miles away. The owner of the condos was willing to exchange our house for one of his condos, but he would not do the exchange for the condo we lived in. He wanted us to move to a different condo for reasons having to do with a higher interest rate he had to pay on the unit he would trade us. This other condo was literally 1 foot away (across a wall that separated Unit D at 1330 from Unit D at 1338). We accepted, and during the actual move, we handed our belongings across the wall that divided the two units. It was one of the hardest moves that we ever made, but worth it since the new Unit D was ours. The own-versus-rent contract meant a great deal of difference to us, and during the 8 years we lived in that condo, we were able to do all the things we had been unable to do before to make it truly a place where we belonged

Joining with another through formal marriage or other commitment (see practice #2, Actualize Your Vows), is like the difference between living at 1338 instead of at 1330. If you don't marry (or strongly commit to one another, however you formalize it), you'll always be stuck in the unit that doesn't belong to you, and you'll never really be assured that you are committed to one another. You may be "living" together, but your tangible commitment to one another will never feel permanent. No matter the rationale that drives the two of you, there is a difference

Be Romantic

Did the romance, so prevalent when you were courting, disappear? What can you do to make it return? Romantic thoughts and actions reap rewards!

et me be honest. At first, I needed to learn more about this practice myself. I think I am now very good at it. I had a decent foundation, having come from a very healthy upbringing, but romancing needed some honing in marriage. Given my experience, I am convinced anyone can learn to be more romantic. You might have to shake off a few things (mainly forgetfulness) that don't help foster romanticism, and you can! Even using the alarm feature on your Fitbit or calendar on your iPhone can play a role in reminding you to be romantic. I guess that doesn't itself seem romantic, but it helps.

Relationships often get into the rut of routine. We do our job, take the kids to school and their swim meets, mow the lawn, paint rooms, watch TV, clean, cook, and on and on it goes. The question throughout all of "living" is where the romance went. Where is the hugging and kissing? Where are the things that showed her/him/they that you really liked them? Have you taken them out to a special dinner or concert lately without other couples along? Talked to them about how much you treasure living with them? Planned something for the future? If plain living seems just too familiar, too workaday, too routine, it's likely time for some romance!

Now, there is romance and then there is *Romance! Romance* actually requires some thought. *Romance* needs to lift you and your partner out of the ordinary. You have to be creative, not only because you may be out of practice, but because whatever you think to do romantically can backfire if not done with your partner totally in mind. Going out to a restaurant they don't like won't work. Tagging along with some friends may not be wise either, because it isn't just the two of you. The secret here is twofold:

- Harken back to what you did when you were romancing one another, then expand on that.

- Separate the romantic things from daily living.

Note: sex is the icing to romance, not the main ingredient (see practice # 33, Sex, Sensuality, and Relationship).

 **Scenes from Our Relationship**

❖ My wife and I work at home, as we are self-employed. One of the more romantic things we do during the summer months is put the top down on our Miata, let the wind blow our hair, and cruise for two or three hours somewhere around the county. We particularly enjoy a nice drive along the ocean. Add in some different conversation than usual, a stop at a local brewery or ice cream store, some steamed clams during a candlelight dinner, and you will have romance cooking.

❖ I happen to play guitar. It seems there is nothing more romantic to my wife than my playing a few tunes for her now and then. I have a wide repertoire, ranging from country and western, folk, and hymns to an occasional old-time rock and roll (I can do a fair rendition of Buddy Holly's "Oh Boy!") And so, after a long day of whatever, we sit in the living room with glasses of wine or kombucha, and I sing a few songs. I usually end with our couple song, "Loving Her Was Easier than Anything I'll Ever Do Again." (see Practice # 1, Have Your Song) Of course, not everyone plays an instrument, but putting some favorite music on and dancing for a while, or other similar activity, isn't that hard to imagine. Sit outside during a beautiful sunset. Sleep outside under the stars. Add some candles and flowers and you have something going. You may have to remind yourself to do so—maybe even schedule it on your calendar or Fitbit. It is like adding plant food to your garden. It just grows better.

I Think My Partner Is Wonderful

What we think about our partner shows. Developing a healthy, rewarding partnership through practices like the many in this book creates a life in which it's easy to have (and to be) a wonderful partner. And once you know how wonderful your partner is, don't keep it a secret!

There is just no question about it—I am crazy about my wife. Sure, we have disagreements now and then, have argued over approaches to business and life, and tell one another to do something this way, not that way. Underlying all this is the constant feeling that I have that she is wonderful, no matter what, and that makes it easy to share spiritual, business, personal, and commitment values that draw us closer and closer as life goes on. It is important to note that this feeling didn't just happen but has grown as we became more open with one another over time. Sure, we made sure we loved one another from the outset, but the "wonder" developed as we processed "stuff" together and built trust in our relationship. We have shared our grief over the death of a daughter and our emotional outpouring during beautiful sunsets on different continents. It's a kind of deep trust in the other person built on years of honestly processing stuff with her, seeing how she approaches life with gusto, and the knowledge that she and I are close partners, truly in sync. It means that I benefit by having a really interesting partner, who sees life a little differently from me. You can make what I feel possible for yourself and your partner, but it takes work on both your parts in building the relationship.

Suppose you respond to this by thinking, "I'm just an average guy who doesn't necessarily think my partner is as wonderful as yours is." There's an easy way to begin: All you need to do is look for the qualities you admire in them and let them know what they are, loud and clear!! "I love your art." "I like the way you treat the kids." "You respond so well to my concerns about my job...or family...or bowling team." "You have a great sense of humor." Once you admire one area out loud, your partner's self-esteem will grow, and you will be even more aware of the things that drew you to them in the first place. Then look for other things you like and nurture those feelings in yourself. Then, look for and act to adjust the things you are not so crazy about in them (or yourself for that matter). Confront these together and see how to make improvements as a joint effort. You will find that their appreciation for you and yours for them grows at the same rate. And when you have those difficulties you will have like any other couple, it will be easier to talk and process (see practice # 14, You Need to Be Able to Process Your Own Stuff First) with them and learn to be better and closer, because you will trust one another more and more. You build a mutual admiration society that will hold you both in good stead (even when you do something stupid).

Scenes from Our Relationship

❖ As I know I've stated elsewhere in the book, I love my wife's ability to process things—on herself as well as between us. Her humor. Her empathy. Her intelligence. Her skills with people and organizations. Her continuous learning. These are all important, but the wonderfulness I feel when I see and think about her is based on her actual being as a person.

I am proud to have worked with her for many years in business and seen how others respect her professionalism. We have written together or edited one another's books and articles. We share a spirituality that she helps me grow through her own reading, personal thoughts, sharing, and teachings. She likes to read to me the things she learns in stories, magazines, online discoveries, TravelZoo, and the like. I like to listen. She isn't just out there leading her own separate life, but rather she is sharing herself and helping me and others grow, too. And I make sure she knows how I feel about her: She is wonderful. It's more than mere respect; she touches me literally and emotionally. That is what I mean by "wonderful." (And I am pretty sure she thinks I am wonderful as well; that's a result you can experience, too.) But you have to work at it.

❖ I have watched her interact with many others—especially women. She is a community builder, but even more so a person who helps others to grow. If it isn't an ACA group she has formed, led, and participated in, then it's some other social justice group, or it's being part of the local "Stitch and Bitch" or Arts Group. It is the numerous personal friends she has who want to take walks with her to discuss life deeply. Rather than staying within herself, she reaches out to others to socialize, but really to help grow and find personal satisfaction. I am in awe of her desire to truly help others as she constantly develops herself. No wonder this adds to my sense of the wonderfulness in her.

Embrace Change to Grow Your Relationship

Change is inevitable in everyone's life. Resisting it is rarely (if ever) successful. When you can learn to embrace change, you almost always find that your relationship is getting better and better.

A viable, healthy relationship is a living, ever-changing phenom-
enon. It grows over time; it never starts out perfect, no matter
how well the courting went. From that point on, it can either grow
and get better, it can remain stagnant, or it can wither and die. Only
the two of you working together can achieve the nirvana so many
couples' desire. It's not what *you* personally want as much as it is what
the two of you want together!

Relationships always change over time because the people you
are and the circumstances you live in together (let alone each of you
separately), inevitably change, and you must adjust together. You
must first recognize the changes taking place within and outside
you—and grow from those experiences as a couple. One friend of
ours remarked that every time her husband fought with her and then
refused to resolve an issue, it was like another brick placed in a wall
they were building between them. Over time, the wall grew, including
decreasing intimacy both sexually and emotionally. Eventually, the
wall was so high it obliterated the relationship. When they finally
broke apart, he was taken by surprise, but he shouldn't have been. If
he had paid attention and held meaningful discussions with his wife,
she would have told him about the Wall. Rather, as changes occurred
in their relationship, he went into hiding (by silence and ignoring
things). He was trying to avoid the change. The result was a divorce.
You don't want to experience this, so here are some thoughts to avoid
having a wall built in your relationship.

No matter how much you dislike change, you have to get used
to it. My old graduate school advisor once proclaimed, "Change
brings conflict, and that isn't necessarily bad." Conflict between
the two of you is almost always necessary to bring about an awareness of change. If you can't accept changes in your marriage, it is

unlikely to survive. This is especially true if one of you recognizes the change and the other does not. Even worse, in an effort to avoid the conflict, you and your partner could settle into a zombie-like state where everyone else guesses that you don't like one another very much. And for the two of you, that detachment creates an "Is this all there is?" feeling.

I happen to be the author of an approach to business known as "The Language of Work Model." It is a highly effective way to organize, implement, and monitor business work effectiveness, because it is based on achieving clarity through a formula for work that anyone can understand and use. The formula succeeds by empowering people to be their very best on their own, as well as in teams. They know one another's' work and its relationship to their own and thus there is far less confusion in their working relationships. With such transparency, change in one area is visible and understandable to people in another area. Working relations are maintained rather than becoming broken apart.

In marriages, we need a similar model, but all models need guidelines to succeed and I have provided many of these in this book. You and your partner need, as do workers in business, clarity in your relationship and its various interactions. To that end, the secret sauce to achieving a great relationship is recognizing that it's a growing process: You come to know and appreciate each other's ways and differences more and more over the entire span of your relationship. You are constantly changing in your understanding of, and reaction to, the other person. You are not becoming versions of one another, but rather understanding, appreciating, and becoming more comfortable with who they are and who they are becoming, a process which is likely to continue your entire time together. Enjoy each phase, because another challenge will surely come, and with it, new opportunities to grow (dammit!).

Each stage of achieving clarity in your relationship requires a *new level* of clarity. Some of the major changes include having a child, refocusing a career, and moving to a new location. Others are facing money issues, grave illness, accidents, infidelity, new demands by families, deaths, existing issues, and the like. Even pandemics.

Having the courage and ability (see practices # 11, You Can't Change The Other Person, and # 14, You Need to be Able To Process Your Own Stuff) to hold meaningful discussions are key practices in dealing with changes like those just mentioned and others. It might be tempting to avoid the discussions. "Why stir up trouble?" or "It's sure to open a can of ugly worms," we think. If you believe in letting sleeping dogs lie, you will be sadly mistaken when the dog wakes up. The actuality is that such discussions, rather than having negative consequences, mostly result in a stronger bond. You learn each time how to be the spouse needed at that time and how to be better at accepting change. As a result, you trust one another more to work through whatever it is that presents itself. You are able to bring up literally any issue because you are assured, based on prior experiences, that all will be resolved. Such honesty causes the air of relationship to clear and the future is always brighter and possible.

Scenes from Our Relationship

❖ Every once in a while, (say, every two to six months), my wife and I deliberately discuss the state of our relationship; we talk about what's working and what needs some improvement. Rather than waiting for a problem to manifest itself (and they do), we forestall a "heat of the moment" response by reaching out to each other to read the barometer of where we are—you might say, a State of the Marriage! This includes all the little—and big—parts of our relationship. How do we feel about the support (or lack of it) we are getting in dimensions like her art, my writing, our community outreach, our interactions with friends, our date night, preparing dinner together, house upkeep and so on. And we always also talk about just how lucky we are to be where we are in life, and especially in being together. We are truly discussing our current relationship and planning for the future. It's kind of like planning a trip, but it's the soul trip of our life together. Whenever we have these discussions, the future seems brighter. We are able to continue to grow our trust and love through it all.

Even though I mentioned a now-and-then schedule to take stock, the most meaningful discussions of relationship should occur whenever one partner feels like they need it. If you have children, and their needs are driving life on a daily basis, you both need to take stock of how that is affecting you as a couple. The way my partner and I look at it is that the discussion is needed when one or the other gets that feeling that we not as close as we were just a while ago. One of us might say, "Something is out of sync. What is it?" You just know there is something amiss, and if you name and discuss it, things can get back on track. It's an uneasy feeling that things could be or used to be better. You just have to say, "Wait a minute, let's name that feeling and hold a discussion!" It's asking one another what has changed and how we need to adjust to it. We always feel better and closer after such discussions.

❖ I used to think that holding a deep discussion with my partner was just another opportunity to get into an argument. Why experience bad feelings by bringing up a topic that will surely lead to conflict? It's taken repeated discussion on many issues to get on the other side of that feeling. My partner and I have learned through concerted effort to hold meaningful discussions; not just argue a point of view that we each hold. As a result, we now discuss anything and come out the other side with workable answers and solutions. We developed a process that works for us. I have a partner with whom I can discuss and resolve anything. And each time we do that, my confidence increases that we like one another all that much more. Combine that with the recognition that change "isn't all that bad," and you find your relationship just getting better and better.

Work to Solution: Don't Just Give In

In a good partnership, both husband and wife understand that communication is a tool to help achieve harmony, and both are willing to do the work to ensure they will each give a little and get a little to arrive at a satisfactory result on any issue.

his may well be the most complex practice in this book; simply because it involves the use of several different (but highly related) practices that all culminate in couples arriving at solutions to their issues. Hang in there with me, and I'll try to make it as straightforward as possible.

Have you ever been in one of those discussions with your partner where you get frustrated at the direction it's going, so you end up saying, "Fine, do it your way"? Or you say, "I give up!" You capitulate. The problem is that the result isn't acceptable. It's a sign that you and your partner may not be mature enough to do the hard work that leads to a mutually satisfactory outcome. One or both of you come away feeling unhappy, dissatisfied, or even dismissed. What's to be done? How do you stick in there until you can both achieve a mutually satisfactory result?

There are several factors involved but let me boil it down to four key ones, two of which are described elsewhere in this book. I'll describe the remaining two below. (If these don't work, you both may need some counseling as well.) The four factors are:

Listening   (practice #13, Listen Well and with Empathy)
Processing   (practice #14, You Need to Be Able to Process Your
             Own Stuff First)
Answering
Arriving at Solution

Other practices, like humor (#3) and change (#11) also contribute to work to solution.

When a couple is discussing a topic in need of a solution to any issue (the kids, what to buy, where to go, who to see, etc.), each partner needs to listen with empathy, process all the information in ways that indicate an understanding, leading to suggested answers, and accepting tradeoffs that will allow meaningful solution(s). By mastering the first two practices and dutifully following the remaining two, both of you will be able to reach a result you both can live with. Since the first two practices have been described elsewhere in the book, we will take a closer look at "answering," and finding solutions in partnership.

I need to say something about men in general when it comes to the topic of answering your partner's questions. I've needed to use some stereotypes in writing this book. It's just "shorthand" to make a point. There are, of course, exceptions. One of those stereotypes is that men are usually more silent and impatient than women. Me, for example, I get silent. I am kind of like one of those old movies about a submarine that decides to "run silent" because the enemy is present. Of course, my wife is not the enemy, so my behavior makes little sense. If that's true of you as well, let me suggest how you can get on the other side of your tendency to avoid answering.

Answer avoidance happens when we think that answering the question will get a reaction we don't want. It's easier to say things like "I don't care," or "You decide, if it's all that important to you." We hope our partner will leave it at that. Sometimes that works, but most times it simply irritates our partner. After enough of these, they may well adopt the posture that they will do what they want since their partner won't commit one way or the other.

Giving up is a form of hiding (the submarine going silent) from the question at hand and nothing more. Once you can accept that it is better to answer the questions, you will both be much happier and much closer to one another. So now whenever I find myself about to say, "Fine," or "I don't care," I stop and tell myself, "Answer the damn question!" And, partner, don't punish him for answering. This is a dialogue time! Time to share information. What's important is that you are talking things out, not punishing one another.

Arriving at a solution first and foremost recognizes that you don't always get everything you want. An agreement in any kind of dispute can be reached by each side making concessions. Remember that the overall goal is to arrive at a solution you can both live with. Couples typically must learn to trust one another's points of view and openly evaluate proposed solutions. Being able to honestly answer your partner is a key component of establishing that trust. Being able to work with their answers helps them trust you. And you must recognize that your partner sometimes has better answers than you do.

Scenes from Our Relationship

❖ We have friends who moved to our state for his job. He likes it here just fine—even after retiring. His wife, though, is not finding the friends and art scene she left. We have watched him recite, "But, it's perfect" each time she suggested they look for another place to live. He's, obviously, not listening or answering to his partner's desires. We managed to avoid this problem. I like country, and my wife loves cities. While driving from Santa Monica, California where we were living, up through Idaho where I grew up, and into Washington State we looked at all kinds of potential relocation opportunities. She wanted to know if I wanted to move back to Idaho, but I assured her it wasn't a priority for me. I could see her breathe a sigh of relief each time I rejected countryside; I had had that experience for 10 years already. We didn't stop looking until we found the perfect compromise between Seattle and Vancouver, B.C. While it is quieter than my wife normally prefers, she has grown to love being close to birds, trees, deer and bunnies, but still within striking distance of cities. She's even describes at times it as living in a Disney movie. Knowing she likes cities; I've been enthusiastic whenever she's suggested a day trip or a getaway to a city like Victoria, B.C.—even NYC.

❖ The circumstances that often lead to my saying, "I don't care!" usually center around whether or not I want to attend certain kinds of functions. If asked to go to an event at the local live performing arts center, I say "I don't care." A trip to the mall the same. A fundraiser, for sure I am, "I don't care!" There are plenty of other social situations that I am ambivalent about. And the truth of the matter is that generally I really don't care one way or the other, but that doesn't excuse my not answering what my wife wants to know my interest in doing or not. In all these I have to catch myself because (1) I do sometimes care, and (2) my partner really deserves to know. Combine this with the fact that more times than not I find myself actually enjoying these events, I should offer a helpful answer rather than derailing my partner. Therefore, I commit myself to and am doing a much better job telling my partner what I really want. Now I feel much better doing so, and I am sure she does too.

Do You Want Me To Coach You on That?

If you've ever had an urge to tell your partner how (in your humble opinion) to do something better or not to do it at all, you might like to know how to avoid seeming to lecture. Coaching is so much more helpful.

I'd like to think I know and can do anything. I used to once joke with my then 7-year old granddaughter that I did, but it didn't take long before they discovered that I didn't know it all. I need help on a number of things, it turns out. It so happens that my partner and I do coaching in our shared business relationship, and so bringing that practice (and its associated change) to our personal relationship is not something new to us. Most relationships don't share such a starting point, but coaching can be learned and practiced by everyone once you accept its value on a continuous basis. We have found that coaching is useful, possible, and not to be ignored in partner nourishing. I learned that from my wife. She had plenty of experience in coaching both professionally and with her many friends, who value her guidance, even before we began to work together.

I saw quickly that coaching can be a fine substitute for honing, correcting, reminding, and/or instructing your partner on things that you believe could be better done another way. Coaching, by the very sound of the word, is a less threatening approach than lecturing or arguing. It helps suggest needed improvement to another person—partner or not—largely because you are not "telling" as much as "guiding." At its heart, coaching is the skillful guiding of another through the learning of useful skills and/or knowledge. It allows for the one being coached to ask for clarity on the path to understanding, and then to practice in whatever it is that one is being coached on. And, it generally comes with a set of rules as to how one coaches.

It might seem a bit of a stretch, but a long time ago I learned how to train my dog to jump through a hoop (not that I would ever ask my wife to do so). In so doing, I had to learn certain behaviorally based principles as to what and how much information to provide at any given time, in what form, and the feedback that would encourage attainment of a desired goal. That could sound complex, but it really isn't. It requires skill, sensitivity, patience, and an understanding of the use of positive reinforcement when specific goals (usually small ones) are met. It should not be attempted casually as it may fail. Not everyone is a natural coach, but virtually everyone can learn to be one. This is all to suggest that if one can learn to teach a dog how to fetch (or not to bite), they can also guide people in how to behave differently.

Scenes from Our Relationship

❖ Others have noted that I am a T-shirt kind of guy. I grew up in Idaho at a time when fashion was hardly on the average person's list of necessities, unless you were a cowboy who needed a large belt buckle. Today my dress code in general is okay, but there are times when I could use a little help, and I don't realize it (for example, when we are going to an event at the local performing arts center, to a funeral, or to an art exhibit). Often, I ask something like, "What's the dress code for this event?" and I get some suggestions from my wife. Or, if I don't think to ask and am dressed in something inappropriate, my partner will say, "Let me coach you on the dress code." I find that expression a nice way of drawing my attention to what I may have overlooked, what she needs to tell me, something where she thinks I could use some help. And it doesn't seem negative or critical when she puts it that way. This no accusatory approach to a sincere desire on her part to help me is so much better than if she had said, "Do you know how unready you look?" On another occasion, she could ask, "May I coach you on what might have been a better response to the question our friend asked about the Middle East?" which is far kinder than, "Here's what you should have said!" It frees me to ask, "What is it that I said and how do you think it could have been put more appropriately?" The same kind of approach works on errors of omission!

All of us make mistakes in what we say or do, and having a partner who can help you, or being a partner who can help their partner, recognize a better way is so much more loving than blaming, castigating, or just being critical. So, the next time you need to say something to your partner, begin with, "May I coach you on that?"

Don't Live in the Past

Repeatedly reminding your partner of unhappy occurrences from the past is pure punishment. It does nothing to make the present and future better. Stick to the present to work on the future.

It is certain that there is no other practice that will eventually lead to the ruination of a relationship than when one or both partners use the past to beat up on the present and future of their relationship. Continually regurgitating past transgressions over and over is simply not useful in resolving anything. "You never support my position on what the kids can and can't do!" "You are always late!" "Why does your friend, Jack, always have to come over?" These kinds of "You" and "Always" statements might make you, the historian, feel good at the time or feel more righteous than your partner. But living in the past does nothing to make your present and future relationship any better.

Living in the past is a state of mind, where one focuses on negative things that our partner may, or may not, have wrought on us. These are affronts that we should be blamed for in the eyes of our partner and can be reused again and again when convenient in an argument. Let's put aside for the moment all those other things that we believe others (family, friends, and colleagues) have done to us, and just focus on our partner.

In one form or another, all of us have experienced living in the past. It takes the form, usually, of your (parent, friend, other) partner reminding you of something you said, or did that was not, in their point of view appropriate or was vindictive in some way. When living in the past is done excessively our relationships go astray. You remind your partner that he forgot your anniversary, you (perhaps in anger) said her parents were not sensitive to your child rearing, they were not supportive of you in some other way(s), and on and on. Some of us do many things right and a few things wrong. Some of us do many things wrong and haven't learned our lesson. Now, while there is value to learning from our past and discussing how to improve, being reminded again and again by others of the need to do better is not so helpful. It serves more as a punishment that can inhibit learning than learning to change.

In terms of the practice of not living in the past, the question is how much is too much? In general, forget the past, and focus on today, this moment. Keep to the present and, if there is an issue right now, resolve it. Now.

Scenes from Our Relationship

Note: My wife's sense of this practice is quite revealing and worthy of your consideration.

❖ Danny is so committed to this practice that he creates a "zone" where old issues cannot be discussed. I found this hard early in our relationship because I am slow to anger. Say something mean? First time, I dismiss it. Second time, I seethe a bit, but try to ignore it. The third time, I blow up! And then I am ready to spew the hated "You always . . ." line.

Living without the opportunity to line up the evidence ("you did this"," you said that"," you never . . .") seemed unfair—at first. But having a partner who has a rule—really a desire—that was initially tough to live with taught me two things: First, don't wait! If I don't like something, I address it right away. And if I do wait 'til the third (or fifth) time to say something, I don't need to review all the past instances. I can just address the one incident—perhaps using the others only for energy. Our relationship isn't a courtroom. I am not there to convict my partner. I am, like him, looking for a solution so we can learn and move on.

Accept Compromise.
It Won't Hurt as Much as You Think

We guys often act as if compromising is somehow a bad thing. In fact, everyone needs to give a little. Besides, life isn't really just about us.

*C*ompromise is:

> *an agreement or a settlement of a dispute that is reached by each side making concessions.*

Or

> *a middle state between conflicting opinions or actions reached by mutual concession or modification.*

Both definitions strike me as a little bit too much. They make compromise sound formal or even bitter. And I can't say I like the word "dispute," even if couples often seem to be disputing something. Mostly, I think that compromise isn't so much about what one person concedes, but rather about what both participants might gain. Compromise can be the source of an optimistic, win-win result, not a pessimistic case in which someone has to lose. Compromise is related to one's attitude and actions towards their partner. Most importantly, compromise is about respect, sensitivity, opportunity, accepting change, and honoring the needs and desires of another. Compromise won't really hurt that much—certainly not as much as we might fear. I have found that if I compromise, I always gain more than I lose.

Scenes from Our Relationship

❖ My partner knows very well that I do not like meetings of any kind. When I do go, I often feel that my fellow participants like to hear themselves talk, instead of listening and then getting something done. This perception isn't, of course, totally true, but meetings do seem to me to be a waste of valuable time. Required to attend, I tolerate them as best I can. When I am the head of such events, I make sure they are brief and to the point. My partner, on the other hand, thrives at meetings and asks that I occasionally attend one with her. So I have learned to compromise when she freely schedules and invites me to museum tours, talks by experts, and social action meetings. When I choose to go with her, I almost always end up enjoying the experience. A lot has to do with the desire to be with her, but it's also the recognition that I might actually learn something and enjoy the experience.

❖ My wife compromises as well. At the beginning of our marriage, my wife didn't like baseball. She had never attended a major league game and did not expect to ruin that record. Growing up, she wasn't particularly enamored of seeing her father and brothers sitting around the TV yelling and screaming at a bunch of men who seemed to be acting randomly. However, when good friends asked us to accompany them to a baseball game, she compromised. Now we go to two or three games a year. It's not surprising that she now knows a few players by name and asks questions about the rules that govern the game. Both parties to a relationship can compromise and, in the end, often learn new things, while also learning to value one another's needs and desires. That is what makes them! Put in other words, if you don't try, you never know what you might be missing.

"And I helped!": Relationship Will Never Be 50/50

You feel really good when you have helped another person. You can also make sure your partner gets that feeling. Men need to learn to ask their partner for help as well as to offer it. And when they give it, thank them.

When I was in my 30s there was a clever ad on TV for a new product known as Shake and Bake. It showed a little girl in the kitchen helping her mother preparing to fry chicken. You rolled the chicken in a plate of breadcrumbs, put them in a fry pan, and voila, you had crispy fried chicken. The clever part of the ad occurred when the little girl exclaimed, in a southern accent, "And I helped!" She didn't really do much, but it made her and her mother happy. It must have felt like a real contribution to that little girl and it gave her mother a thrill to hear her.

I can't imagine there is any relationship that is exactly 50/50. Relationships involve so many aspects of being and doing for oneself and for the other that any attempt to make it equal will fall short. Equality is not in the cards for a number of reasons. Your contribution and your partner's contribution will always be some other numbers that add up to 100. You may be giving 60% some of the time, and another time your partner may be giving 65%. The relationship between you—who does what and why—is much easier to live with than any numerical value in your mind arbitrarily assigned by each partner. Friends of ours, where the husband "cannot boil water," have found it easy for the wife to do all the cooking, while he takes up the slack in other ways. Still, I know other couples where the man does all the cooking. The attitude you have about your partner and their attitude about you are much more important than any accounting exercise.

One of the reasons there is inequality in a partnership is the perception that the other person should do such and such because they are better at it than you are. The notion that the partner is better at cleaning toilets, therefore they should do them all the time, is nuts. Anyone can clean a toilet, or whatever is plaguing your relationship and causing resentment. Open yourself to the possibilities of what you can learn, determine the effect it will have on your partnership, and think how good you might feel that you contributed to something that made your partner happy.

Scenes from Our Relationship

❖ My partner and I know that we can't achieve equity, so we don't try. Rather, we each appreciates what the other does. If the task at hand is more one-sided than it should be, an expression of, "How could I help?" indicates a willingness to balance things out. Whenever my wife (or I) does just a little part of something that the other of us is doing, such as painting the deck or building a fire, I say, "And you helped!" Or if it's framing artwork or making an elaborate dinner, she says, "And you helped!" It's a nice way to express recognition of our mutual efforts, as minor or even corny as that may seem. Letting each other be involved makes us both feel better about ourselves and one another.

❖ Last week I decided (after many years) to paint the unfinished walls of our garage. It's the kind of task that I find easy to accomplish and quite comfortable doing on my own. I patched holes, taped cabinets borders, rolled lots of paint, and in general moved the project along quiet efficiently. In other words, I could have done this task all on my own, but I know better than to do so. As I went along doing this and that, I asked for my partner's input on color, what was to stay or be gotten rid of, and when the final coat was applied, her keen eye on spots that were missed. "She Helped!" and knows that I value her input. She has now suggested—being the artist that she is—some artwork to adorn a couple of the garage walls. What was the boring garage project, now has our personal touches as an extension of the beautiful inside our home.

Stay Close to One Another

You and your partner have chosen to have a life together. By that commitment you agree to become together more than either of you is separately. Always remember that.

Lying close to one another can be a particularly important feature of life if you are lucky enough to have a willing partner. There are other, more intimate versions of being with one another, but this one is the closest I can think of as a way of saying, "I like being around you and I trust you."

For those who think that lying close should naturally lead to sex, I'd say you are missing both the opportunity and real value of simple, nondemanding physical contact. Lying close without sex brings feelings of safety and serenity that can benefit the relationship and your own psychological well-being. It may take a while to achieve that with your partner, especially if it is a new behavior. You may have to repeatedly assure them that you just want to cuddle. And of course, you need to keep your word.

Lying close, in my terms, takes different forms and can occur at different times of the day and night. Sitting in the same lounge chair and watching a movie is one version. Lying back to back at night or nap time or holding hands at first light of the day are others. Sitting and touching bodies next to one another in a church pew or sitting side by side in a restaurant (rather than across a table) are others. Holding hands during a movie. Putting your arm around your partner. You are saying, in these many ways, to the world, but more importantly to each other, that you enjoy one another's company. Discomfort at any of these actions may be a sign that other things are amiss in the relationship. Then you need to talk and to do things to improve what keeps you physically, let emotionally apart. Being close is the physical manifestation of love.

Scenes from Our Relationship

❖ As I have grown older, I don't sleep as well as used to. Back in the day I could easily sleep the night away. On reflection, I may have been missing a lot! Because I now have occasion to wake during the night, say at 2:00 a.m., I have discovered that I can ease my random thoughts by simply reaching over to the other side of the bed and touching my partner's arm or shoulder. She doesn't mind and often then reaches to hold my hand. In the darkness of the night, all becomes well, and I am then able to go off to sleep once again.

❖ Holding hands is an act of kindness and togetherness that my wife and I treasure. You can find us on a walk anywhere holding hands. Going down the aisle at church, in a theatre watching a movie, early in the morning lying in bed, and certainly in times of grief at the death of a child, parent, or other loved one. We both think of this simple physical act as a barometer of how things are going in our relationship. When the handholding is not frequent, we want to know why and talk to discover its origin and then a solution. We go back to holding hands again. My wife and I have come to greatly value just being physically close. I think we sense our inevitable end, so over time we have gotten even closer.

Put Down the Toilet Seat

The need for this—and the benefit—will be clear to those who choose to be mindful of others.

Nothing more need be said, gents! Put the toilet seat down after you have used it!

# # #

A Delicious Recipe for Men
(who don't cook)
To Prepare for Their Partner

Salmon Cakes

Ingredients Needed

- 14.75 oz can of Salmon
- Progresso Italian Breadcrumbs
- One Small to Medium size Onion
- 2 Eggs
- Salt and Pepper

Utensils

- 12" or larger frying pan
- Spatula (not metal)
- Olive (or Vegetable) Oil
- Medium Mixing Bowl
- Wooden Spoon (or metal one if that is all you have)

Recipe Instructions

1. Open the can of Salmon with a can opener. Place the lid back on the can and drain the liquid in the salmon can into the sink.

2. Place the salmon in the mixing bowl and break it apart with a wooden spoon so that it is completely separated.

3. Cut up half the onion (a medium sized one) into small bite sizes and place it in the mixing bowl and stir with the salmon until consistent.

4. Crack and put two eggs into the salmon bowl. Mix the salmon and onions with the eggs until consistent.

5. Now comes the tricky part. Pour about a half cup of breadcrumbs into your salmon mixture and stir until consistent. The mixture should bind together well enough so that when you flatten a ball of it about half the size of a hamburger patty it sticks together like a hamburger patty would.

6. Turn on a burner to medium heat, place the skillet on it, and pour in some olive oil enough to lightly cover the bottom of it. Get it hot over medium heat or a little less.

7. Make four 3" size patties of the salmon mix, place them in the skillet and cook slowly on one side (probably 3 minutes) until slightly brown, turn over and cook until the other side is brown. BUT NOT TOO MUCH THAT THEY DRY OUT!

8. Take them out and place on a dish. Serve with tartar sauce or you can mix equal amounts of mayo and sweet relish and you have your own sauce.

9. Buy or make a salad and you have a meal

10. Don't forget the napkins!

Practices Progress Checklist

(See Following Pages)

Practice		Have Mastered	Will Practice	Not Possible For Me
1.	Have Your Song			
2.	Actualize Your Vows: "My Connubials"			
3.	Humor in Relationship			
4.	Start the Day Together: Knock Three Times			
5.	As Aretha Said, **R-e-s-p-e-c-t**			
6.	For Heavens' Sake, Hold Your Partner's Hand			
7.	Pitch in			
8.	You Can Ask for Help			
9.	Viva La Brain Difference			
10.	Praise Works			
11.	You Can't Change the Other Person			
12.	Be Honest: Not Judgmental			
13.	Listen Well and with Empathy; Don't Offer Solutions			
14.	You Need to Be Able to Process Your Own S(tuff) First			
15.	Sorry: Doing vs Saying			
16.	Acknowledge Moody Times:			
17.	Recognize that Your Partner Has a Life of Their Own			

Practice	Have Mastered	Will Practice	Not Possible For Me
18. There Is Nobody Better to Spend Time With			
19. Avoid Nitpicking			
20. What Can You be Relied on to Do?			
21. Flowers Now and Then			
22. We'll Never Run Out of Things to Talk About			
23. Acknowledge Your Partner's Opinions			
24. A Little Publicity in Your Marriage!			
25. Your Appearance: Listen to Your Partner			
26. Expand Your Horizons Together			
27. There's Value in Having a Spiritual Side			
28. Words Count			
29. Money, Money, Money			
30. The Big Three: Periods, Pregnancy, and Menopause			
31. A Day (or part of it) for Us			
32. Be Kind			
33. Sex, Sensuality, and Relationship			
34. Learn to Read the Nonverbal			

Practice	Have Mastered	Will Practice	Not Possible For Me
35. Have a Few Really Good Couple Friends			
36. Do Something for Humanity			
37. Patience: She Is Only Going to Be Ready When She Is Ready			
38. Relatives, Neighbors and Friends			
39. Putting Your Partner in the Conversation			
40. Commitment Is Stronger than "Non-Commitment"			
41. Be Romantic			
42. I think My Partner Is Wonderful			
43. Embrace (Don't Resist) Change to Grow Your Relationship			
44. Work to Solution: Don't Just Give In			
45. Do You Want Me to Coach You on That?			
46. Don't Live in the Past			
47. Accept Compromise. It's Won't Hurt as Much as You Think			
48. "And I Helped!" Relationship Will Never Be 50/50			
49. Stay Close to One Another			
50. Put Down the Toilet Seat			

Post Practice
Write Your Relationship Story

My Relationship Story:
A Sample from The Author

I am going to describe the history of my relationships by first looking backward, then the present (then, circa 1990), and finally forward into time. In that way I will capture what I initially entered marital relationships in the way of practices, what I came to realize and finally, what I achieved by paying attention to the practices described in this book.

Like many a young person (I was 25) entering into a relationship that culminated in marriage, I initially had little idea of what made for a good marriage. In my case, my father died when I was seven, so I did not have much time to see how my mother and father related to one another. I was much too young to even know what I might be looking for in the way of practices that made for a good relationship. As a kid, it was naturally more about me than what my parents were doing. I didn't ask myself, such questions as: "Did they process well?" "How did they treat one another?" "How did he show that he cared for her?" "When they argued, what happen next?" I did not learn much of anything about relationships watching my parents.

Furthermore, there was no extended family around to see what they did either. My brothers and sisters were all older than me, and even their marriages were distant, although some lived nearby. Any idea of relationships to me was like looking at a house a mile away. I had no idea of what's going on inside and what I would do if you lived there. Thus, when I got married the first time, I was pretty much on my own to figure it out. I was lucky to have at least come from a family that itself had a healthy and loving environment. I brought that to my marriage with pretty much a complete stranger who had their own experiences. Most of us, as they say, have to wing it!

During the first time I was married, I did a pretty fair job of it, but I, of course, made mistakes. I think I was fairly defensive, didn't like to be told to do this or that, and perhaps did not learn how to process effectively as I should have. Still, it was a good enough life for me and my partner, although it did not work out as a forever-life relationship. We parted amicably, each aware that we could have done better. A shortlist of my short comings included practices I identify in the book as Viva La Brain Difference, Praise Works, You Can't Change the other Person, Sorry: Doing vs Saying, Acknowledging Moody Times, Words Count, Learn To Read The Nonverbals, Embracing Change, Work To Solutions, among perhaps others. That may seem like a lot, and it is, but coming to realize these became benchmarks for improvement as I went forth into a second life for me at the age of 51.

At the end of my marriage I happen to receive a job offer in another state. This afforded me the opportunity to kind of start life again. It was there that I started to date and soon discovered a relationship that I approached in a much different way than I had the first time. After all, I had a better idea of what marriage was and should be based largely on the first experience. I spent more time during dating on two things: (1) what characteristics did I desire as in a partner, and (2) what did I need to improve about myself as a partner? Those practices that I listed previously became my goals for improvement.

What I wanted in another person was a rather shortlist, but vital. Chief among those were practice # 14 (Process Your Own Stuff First) and # 49 (Stay Close). Add to these two practices others that were important to my new partner (as we discussed before marriage), made for a nice set of practices we could hone together. Thus, we were entering our new relationship with clear expectations of relationship and relationship building far greater than the first time for either one of us. We would be committing ourselves to building a strong, in-sync relationship.

It seems to me that the most important practice we worked on from the very beginning was reinforcing the notion that each of us had to be able to process our own issues first and very effectively, because only then were we able to process together. And, of course processing together often brought into play other practices, such as listening with empathy, realizing you can't change the other person, acknowledging moody times, realizing they have a life of their own, and so on. What we did was set out to make our life together really work, be fun, and let each other grow in our separate talents. In our case we formed a business and we realized in working together that the client is the one to be served far above our individual approach to solving business problems. In being life-partners, we realized that our relationship was more important than anything else. So we kept the target clear and life just got better and better year after year. It took work, attention of particular practices, but we did it. It's hard to express just how great it is now.

I learned a number of practices from my partner that I want to recognize and note their importance in helping us build our relationship. The first practice she taught me was # 13, Listen well and With Empathy: Don't Offer Solutions. You see, like most males, when I heard my partner describe some issue she was grappling with, my immediate reaction was to offer a solution. Turns out, that is not what she was looking for. Rather, she wanted me to first wait and hear her out before commenting, and second, offer some empathy through words that demonstrates that I heard her and felt for her conundrum. Once I did this, I found that understanding her need allowed her to process and resolve it. This requires remembering Practice # 11, You Can't Change the Other Person.

Another practice, Viva La Brain Difference came to me because of a professional colleague. This guy was an expert in Right Brain/Left Brain and he not only analyzed me for what my dominance was, but help me realize what my partner's dominate attributes were. Thus, I learned how to relate to her in terms of where she was coming from during discussions, plans, and preferences. Then, how to come to better communicate between the two of us. I became much less adamant that my way was the best and only way.

Another important practice I learned from my partner was # 45, Do You Want Me to Coach You On That? I admit, and she knows me well, that I don't like to be told what to do. However, every one of us at times needs to be told something. Instead of her telling me what to do, she starts out by saying, "Do you mind if I coach you on that?" Somehow that puts a softer touch on what's coming, and I am ready and willing to listen and most likely do it. You just have to try it to believe it.

Let me close with # 49, Stay Close To One Another. It seems to me that no matter what positive or negative things we do to one another, realizing that we need to stay close to one another is critical. We are not here to be better than our partner, always have to win the argument, do things only our way, and so forth. Rather, we are here together to build a loving relationship. I stay close to her, and she does to me, by paying attention to several of the other practices. We have, for example, a spiritual life, do things for humanity together, have close friends, I think she is wonderful, we don't live in the past, and on and on. Practice does make perfect.

In closing, here is an outline to which you can write your own story much as I have done here. When you are clear on that story, consider sharing with your partner and having meaningful discussion on further building your relationship.

1. What did I enter my current relationship knowing about relationship in general?

2. Where I am currently in my relationship? What have I learned? What more do I need to learn?

3. What will I commit to work on to enhance and reach the kind of relationship we desire?

Photo Credits

The author's gratitude for photo resourcing made possible through Buffer.com, including Upsplash, Pexels, and Pixabay. Attributions for each photo is cited with much appreciation.

Additional Information and Resources

See the author's website

thegoodhusband.net

for additional practices, to ask questions of the author,
and view related podcasts and resources.